Endangered Wildlife and Plants of the World

Volume 1
ABU–BIR

Marshall Cavendish

New York • London • Toronto • Sydney

Marshall Cavendish Corporation
99 White Plains Road
Tarrytown, NY 10591-9001

Created by Brown Partworks Ltd
Editor: Anne Hildyard
Associate Editors: Paul Thompson, Amy Prior
Design: Whitelight
Picture Research: Helen Simm
Index Editor: Kay Ollerenshaw
Production Editor: Matt Weyland

Library of Congress Cataloging-in-Publication Data

Endangered wildlife and plants of the world
p.cm.
Includes bibliographical references (p.).
ISBN 0-7614-7194-4 (set)
ISBN 0-7614-7195-2 (vol. 1)
1. Endangered species--Encyclopedias. I. Marshall Cavendish Corporation.

QH75.E68 2001
333.95'22'03--dc21
99-086194

Printed in Malaysia
Bound in the United States of America
07 06 05 04 03 02 01 00 7 6 5 4 3 2 1

Photo Credits

Cover: Still Pictures; David McNew
Title page: Oxford Scientific Films; Deni Brown
Contents: Heather Angel 15: Bruce Coleman Ltd; Dr P Evans
14, Luiz Claudio Marigo 12, Hans Reinhard 13: Natural
History Photographic Agency; Anthony Bannister 11, Stephen
Dalton 19: Daniel Heuchlin 17: Hugh Nourse 18: Still
Pictures; Michel Gunther 20

A-Z Botanical: Yves Tzaud 47
Biofotos: Heather Angel 50
California Native Plant Society: S P Rae 140, Mike Ross 139
J. Cancolosi Peter Arnold, Inc. 136
Gerald D Carr: 23, 24, 26
Cheeseman 65
Bruce Coleman Ltd.: Steven C Kaufman 28, Luiz Claudio
Margio 63
Corbis: Galen Rowell 38
Sylvia Cordaiy Photo Library: Anthony Bloomfield 97
Ron Garrison 41, 42, 61, 85, 87, 124, 128
David Haring 91

P. La Tourette 33
Life File: Bob Harris 80,
Robert & Linda Mitchell 132
Natural History Photographic Agency: Anthony Bannister 52,
Nigel J Dennis 51
Oxford Scientific Films: Deni Bown 48, 55, 57, Daniel Cox
115, Daniel Heuchlin 73, Tim Jackson 54
Still Pictures: Roland Seitre 74
Hans Pfletschinger 76,77
Daphne Pritchard: 49
E.S. Ross 131
Warren Thomas: 43, 60, 67, 99
Merlin D. Tuttle /Bat Conservation International 109, 112
D. Wechsler 108
G Ziesler 79
Zoological Society of San Diego 68, 69, 70,84, 96, 99, 118,
121, 122

Cover: A bighorned sheep. Still Pictures: David McNew
Title page: *Aloe rauhii*. Oxford Scientific Films: Deni Brown

FOREWORD

Forty years ago the term *endangered species* was rarely heard. Now it has become a common phrase in our vocabulary. Even though there have been volumes of material produced pertaining to this subject, the concept and many of the facts of endangerment are still poorly understood. Opinions on the subject are widely divergent, ranging from a desire by some people for unrestricted exploitation of the environment (with humans first, last, and always) to an inflexible policy of protection (without exception) for every species, regardless of the consequences. As with most things in life, enlightened compromise is usually the most sensible approach. To better understand the present situation of wildlife on this planet, we must put it in perspective.

Life probably began around 3.5 billion years ago and has continued to the present. During this incredible span of history, literally millions—if not billions—of life-forms have evolved here: species and subspecies, families, and genera have risen to their fullest potential, fallen into decline, and become extinct. All these events happened through natural causes. The name of the game has always been survival and the perpetuation of the species. Nature is an unsympathetic and demanding master. Each species has had to cope with nature's demands and compete with other species in order to reproduce and perpetuate its own kind. Failing to accomplish this, it disappears and is gone forever.

The powerful effects of competition between species for food, water, light, or simply a place to nest and reproduce must be understood. Since change—that is, evolution—is constant, competitive battles for survival result in some life-forms evolving in ways that give them distinct advantages over others. Therefore, the life-forms we find around us today are the successful survivors in this long, long chain of evolution. Until the advent of our species, Homo sapiens, all the forces that

produced changes and extinctions were natural and happened by chance. Once humans began to control and alter their surroundings, however, the impact on the environment was dramatic. For the first time in this long, 3.5-billion-year adventure, people became a key part of the equation for determining species survival.

Humans change the environment to suit themselves, and rarely are such changes compatible with the needs of other species. Although this fact is evident today, only a few generations ago it was not so obvious. It is easy for us to look back in time and condemn prior generations for their selfish exploitation of this planet, but this would be unfair. We cannot judge yesterday's world with today's understanding. For example, it would have been difficult to convince Lewis and Clark in 1806 that there could ever be an end to the great forests of the Pacific Northwest. No one could have convinced early explorers that the vast herds of American bison they encountered would one day be near extinction, and we could not have convinced 19th-century whalers of the plight of today's whales.

The common belief until the middle of the 20th century was that Earth's resources were unlimited. Today we know better. Witness the near extinction of the blue whale, or the diminishing amount of untouched, old-growth forest that is just a tiny fraction of what it once was. Human beings have used a seemingly endless variety of methods to harm the environment, until the severe alteration of species' populations and habitats has now reached alarming levels. Destroying habitat, however, is not the only problem. Humanity has also been polluting and poisoning what remains.

Within this picture of gloom and doom, we must remember that there is always hope for the present and room for faith in the future. When nature is given a chance, its recuperative powers are astounding. For example, there are a number of species living today numbering in the thousands that were once reduced to a tiny fraction of their original number. Once people gave them protection and carefully managed them, nature was again able to work wonders. A classic example of this is the Père David deer from China, which was once reduced to four animals but today numbers in the hundreds. The gray whale from the west coast of North America was pushed nearly to extinction and now numbers in the thousands. The golden lion tamarin from Brazil was reduced to less than 200 animals and has made a spectacular comeback.

Humans have the ability to preserve what they choose, and they usually choose what they understand and value most. That which is unfamiliar is often ignored. Therefore, it is imperative that every avenue to educate our children be explored, and that they be taught to appreciate and value our fellow travelers on the planet Earth.

If humanity can be motivated to protect and nurture the world, old habits of exploitation and destruction can be minimized. However, it is not practical to accomplish this goal by uncompromising protection at any cost. For example, in some poor areas of the world where people struggle just to survive, it is difficult to convince a village of farmers that it must protect animals such as leopards just because they are endangered species. Since this animal is a habitual carnivore, it kills the goats, dogs, and chickens of the farmers. However, if these villagers can learn to control how many leopards they hunt without jeopardizing the entire species population, and also properly protect their domestic animals, they can continue to benefit from this former domestic enemy by harvesting its valuable products, such as fur. The farmers would then turn a detriment into a valuable asset. This would result in control of poaching and assure a viable population of an irreplaceable species. The village members would have an economic reason to help end poaching and actually save this local predator from extinction. This is called pragmatic—or common sense—conservation.

The same principles apply to plants. Civilization's insatiable demand for wood has resulted in the decimation of countless square miles of forest. It has been estimated that we are losing the equivalent of an area the size of the state of Florida each year in the destruction of tropical rain forests. The end result is disastrous. Much of what was once lush rain forest has now become nearly a biological desert. To restore these rain forests would take well over 100 to 200 years. Some species have been given protection, but often too little too late. For example, the California redwoods have been given some protection, but there is only a tiny fraction of old growth forest remaining. The Chilean larch, which takes almost 15 years to approach maturity, has been decimated to a sad remnant. In addition, almost all the tropical hardwoods are threatened. There are some bright spots in the picture, and some efforts are being made to protect what is left, though not nearly enough. For example, an Asian hardwood such as teak is now being grown domestically, and this will take the pressure off its wild population.

Endangered Wildlife and Plants of the World is a substantial step forward in education and enlightenment. It aims to familiarize readers with those jeopardized species that, in many cases, are hanging in the balance. By knowing of them, appreciating them, and understanding them, perhaps we, as concerned human beings, can take one more step toward preserving them.

Warren D. Thomas, D.V.M.
Taos, New Mexico
Warren Thomas served as director of the Los Angeles Zoo in California from 1974 to 1991.

CONTRIBUTORS AND ACKNOWLEDGMENTS

EDITORIAL CONSULTANTS

BIRDS
Steve Wylie, Executive Director/CEO
  Oklahoma City Zoological Park, Oklahoma
Steve Swaby, Natural History Museum,
  London, England
Megan Cartin

REPTILES AND AMPHIBIANS
Edward J. Maruska, Executive Director
  Cincinnati Zoological park, Ohio

FISH
Megan Cartin

MAMMALS
Robert G. Barnes, Curator of Mammals,
  Los Angeles Zoo, California
Michael Dee, Curator of Mammals,
  Los Angeles Zoo, California
Warren D. Thomas, D.V.M,
  New Mexico
Michael J. Weedon

INSECTS
Michael J. Weedon, Natural History Museum,
  London, England

PLANTS
John Akeroyd, Botanist,
  Wiltshire, England

GENERAL
Bobbie Jo Kelso, TRAFFIC International,
  Cambridge, England
Megan Cartin

CONTRIBUTORS

Kelvin Boot, Head of Education,
  National Marine Aquarium, Plymouth, England
Daniel F. Brunton Consulting Services, Ottawa,
  Ontario, Canada
Megan Cartin
Eric A. Christenson, Sarasota, Florida
Martin Gibbons, The Palm Centre, Ham,
  England
Edward O. Guerrant, Conservation Director,
  The Berry Botanical Garden, Portland, Oregon
Tim Harris
Chuck Hubbuch, Fairchild Tropical Garden,
  Miami, Florida
Rick Imes, North Ferrisburg, Vermont
Kenneth D. Jones, Botanical Curator, St. George
  Village Botanical Garden, U.S. Virgin Islands
Edward J. Maruska, Cincinnati Zoological Park,
  Ohio
Chris Mattison
Robert J. Meinke, Department of Botany and Plant
  Pathology, Oregon State University, Corvallis,
  Oregon
Sara Oldfield, Fauna and Flora Preservation
  Society, Cambridge, England
Christina Oliver, Natural History Museum,
  London
J. Mark Porter, Rancho Santa Ana Botanic
  Garden, Claremont, California
Paula Power and Kathryn Kennedy, U.S. Fish and
  Wildlife Service, San Marcos, Texas
Daphne Pritchard, The Euphorbiaceae Study
  Group, Warrington, Cheshire, England
Fred Rumsey, Department of Botany,
  Natural History Museum,
  London, England

Gordon Rutter, Botanic Gardens,
    Edinburgh, United Kingdom
Adrian Seymour, School of Biological Sciences,
    University of Bristol, England
Salma Shalla, Consultant in Aquaculture and
    Marine Ecology, Isle of Man
Warren D. Thomas, D.V.M
Nicholas J. Turland, Flora of China Project,
    Missouri Botanical Garden
Tom Ward, Manager, Dana Greenhouse,
    The Arnold Arboretum of Harvard University,
    Massachusetts
Eddie Watkins, Ecology and Evolutionary Biology
    of Ferns, Iowa
G. Thomas Watters, Ohio Biological Survey &
    Aquatic Ecology Laboratory
Michael J. Weedon, Natural History Museum,
    London, England
Qiaoping Xiang, Herbarium Institute of Botany,
    Chinese Academy of Sciences, Beijing

ACKNOWLEDGMENTS

The editor would like to thank the following people
and organizations for their help in the preparation
of this work:

John Akeroyd
Megan Cartin
Mike Grant, Royal Horticultural Society, England
Fred Rumsey, The Natural History Museum,
    England
Nicholas J. Turland

The Center for Plant Conservation,
    Missouri Botanical Garden

Many of the bird species accounts were checked
and updated by staff at BirdLife International,
Cambridge, England, which is the leading
authority on the status of the world's birds.

A READER'S GUIDE TO ENDANGERED WILDLIFE AND PLANTS OF THE WORLD

Endangered Wildlife and Plants of the World is arranged in alphabetical order by each animal's or plant's commonly used English name. However, some plants do not have common names; therefore some plants are organized according to their scientific name. For example, under the general heading "ferns," there are several species that do not have common names, these are listed alphabetically using their Latin name. Sometimes a species will have several common names, which may vary from country to country, or they may have locally evolved names. Alternate common names are shown in parentheses. The reader can easily locate a plant or animal without referring to the index. Some related species are in separate places; for instance, cachorritos are part of the killifish family, but the cachorritos entry is found under "C" while the rest of the killifish can be found under "K."

There are ten essays at the end of Volume 12 that discuss various problems related to the endangerment of plants and animals.

SELECTION OF SPECIES

The species listed in *Endangered Wildlife and Plants of the World* are those threatened in various ways with extinction. The primary sources of information regarding endangerment are the U.S. Fish and Wildlife Service, and the Red Lists compiled by IUCN–The World Conservation Union. *The IUCN Red List of Threatened Animals* includes 5,500 species from around the world that are threatened with extinction. All known species of birds and mammals have been included, and 25 percent of mammal species and 11 percent of bird species are classified as being threatened with extinction. Of the reptile, amphibian, and fish

species that have been assessed, it is estimated that 20 percent of reptiles are threatened, 25 percent of amphibians, and 34 percent of fish. *The IUCN Red List of Threatened Plants* includes around 34,000 species facing extinction, which represents 12.5 percent of the world's flora.

The criteria for inclusion of species rests on data from two lists. ESA indicates data compiled by the U.S. Fish and Wildlife Service under the authority of the Endangered Species Act. IUCN indicates the World Conservation Union. A brief description of the two organizations can be found on pages 9 to 10.

INDEX

There are three separate ways in the Index Volume (Volume 13) to allow readers to find the entry they require by looking up either the common name, scientific name, or the geographical area where the species is found. Around 1,400 species and subspecies of animals and plants are indexed and cross-referenced. For example, a species such as the African Wild Ass would appear in the Comprehensive Index under African Wild Ass, and Ass; it would appear in the Geographic Index under Africa, and Mammals, and in the Scientific Index under *Equus africanus* sp.

Volume 1 to 12 each include a volume index.

ENTRIES

After the common name, the plant's or animal's scientific name follows in parentheses. Either one or two status bars follow, indicating ESA classification and IUCN classification. These are color coded according to the degree of endangerment. Exceptions do occur, for instance, the bobcat has no status bar, because it is no longer at risk of extinction. It was included to show that conservation and protection programs have been effective in halting the decline of the species. The status bars are followed by a color panel giving the taxonomic classification of the species. This usually includes class, order, and family, although this may vary for plants, depending on the taxonomic information available.

PHYSICAL DESCRIPTION

A brief, physical description, where appropriate, gives height, weight, diet, reproductive method, habitat, and range. Description of plants includes stem height, leaf measurement, pollination method, flower size, and color. Where information is not available, the description indicates "unknown." Imperial measurements are given, with metric equivalents in parentheses.

MAPS

Each species has a map showing the current range of the species and usually its former range before its population decline. There are some exceptions; for instance, whales and some sharks have such an enormous range spanning so much of the world that a map would not be of any help to the reader. Other species, such as beetles, insects, and butterflies, do not have status bars, descriptions, or maps because there are so many species discussed within one entry. Where many species inhabit an area, the maps may refer to more than one entry.

MULTIPLE ENTRIES

Occasionally species are grouped together in a multiple entry. If they share a common status classification and similar description, this information will only be given once, however, if the status classification differs from species to species, each species will have a separate status.

Each entry ends with the name of the author; in the case of multiple entries that have all been written by the same person, the author's name will be at the end of the final entry.

Some entries have a "See also" reference at the end to direct the reader to other entries in the set with relevant information about related endangered species.

ADDITIONAL MATERIALS

There is a glossary in each volume of the set including a core list of terms employed throughout this publication along with additional terms from the entries in that volume.

The Index Volume contains a standard bibliography as well as a list of wildlife refuges in the U.S. and Canada. There is also a list of private wildlife organizations that readers can contact for additional information.

ESA and IUCN

In this set of endangered animals and plants, each species, where appropriate, is given an ESA status and an IUCN status. The sources consulted to determine the status of each species are the Endangered Species List maintained by the U.S. Fish and Wildlife Service and the Red Lists compiled by IUCN–The World Conservation Union, which is a worldwide organization based in Switzerland.

ENDANGERED SPECIES ACT

The Endangered Species Act (ESA) was initially passed by the U.S. Congress in 1973, and reauthorized in 1988. The aim of the ESA is to rescue species that are in danger of extinction due to human action and to conserve the species and their ecosystems. Endangered plants and animals are listed by the U.S. Fish and Wildlife Service (USFWS), which is part of the Department of Interior. Once a species is listed, the USFWS is required to develop recovery plans, and ensure that the threatened species is not further harmed by any actions of the U.S. government or U.S. citizens. The act specifically forbids the buying, selling, transporting, importing, or exporting of any listed species. It also bans the taking of any listed species in the U.S. and its territories, on both private and public lands. Violators can face heavy fines or imprisonment. However, the ESA requires that the protection of the species is balanced with economic factors.

The ESA recognizes two categories of risk for species:

Endangered: A species that is in danger of extinction throughout all or a significant part of its range.

Threatened: A species that is likely to become endangered in the foreseeable future.

RECOVERY

Recovery takes place when the decline of the endangered or threatened species is halted or reversed, and the circumstances that caused the threat have been removed. The ultimate aim is the recovery of the species to the point where it no longer requires protection under the act.

Recovery can take a long time. Because the decline of the species may have occurred over centuries, the loss cannot be reversed overnight. There are many factors involved: the number of individuals of the species that remain in the wild, how long it takes the species to mature and reproduce, how much habitat is remaining, and whether the reasons for the decline are clear cut and understood. Recovery plans employ a wide range of strategies that involve the following: reintroduction of species into formerly occupied habitat, land aquisition and management, captive breeding, habitat protection, research, population counts, public education projects, and assistance for private landowners.

SUCCESS STORIES

Despite the difficulties, recovery programs do work, and the joint efforts of the USFWS, other federal and state agencies, tribal governments, and private landowners have not been in vain. Only seven species, less than 1 percent of all the species listed between 1968 and 1993, are now known to be extinct. The other 99 percent of listed species have not been lost to extinction, and this confirms the success of the act.

There are some good examples of successful recovery plans. In 1999, the peregrine falcon, the bald eagle, and the Aleutian goose were removed from the endangered species list. The falcon's numbers have risen dramatically. In 1970, there were only 39 pairs of falcons in the United States. By 1999, the number had risen to 1,650 pairs. The credit for the recovery goes to the late Rachel

Carson, who highlighted the dangers of DDT, and also to the Endangered Species Act, which enabled the federal government to breed falcons in captivity, and took steps to protect their habitat.

Young bald eagles were also successfully translocated into habitat that they formerly occupied, and the Aleutian Canada goose has improved due to restoration of its habitat and reintroduction into former habitat.

IUCN–THE WORLD CONSERVATION UNION

The IUCN (International Union for Conservation of Nature) was established in 1947. It is an alliance of governments, governmental agencies, and nongovernmental agencies. The aim of the IUCN is to help and encourage nations to conserve wildlife and natural resources. Organizations such as the Species Survival Commission is one of several IUCN commissions that assesses the conservation status of species and subspecies globally. Taxa that are threatened with extinction are noted and steps are taken for their conservation by programs designed to save, restore, and manage species and their habitats. The Survival Commission is committed to providing objective information on the status of globally threatened species, and produces two publications: the *IUCN Red List of Threatened Animals*, and the *IUCN Red List of Threatened Plants*. They are compiled from scientific data and provide the status of threatened species, depending on their existence in the wild and threats that undermine that existence. The lists for plants and animals differ slightly.

The categories from the *IUCN Red List of Threatened Animals* used in *Endangered Wildlife and Plants of the World* are as follows:

Extinct: A species is extinct when there is no reasonable doubt that the last individual has died.

Extinct in the wild: A species that is known only to survive in captivity, well outside its natural range.

Critically endangered: A species that is facing an extremely high risk of extinction in the wild in the

immediate future.

Endangered: A species that is facing a very high risk of extinction in the wild in the near future.

Vulnerable: A species that is facing a high risk of extinction in the wild in the medium-term future.

Lower risk: A species that does not satisfy the criteria for designation as critically endangered, endangered, or vulnerable. Species included in the lower risk category can be separated into three subcategories:

Conservation dependent: A species that is part of a conservation program. Without the program, the species would qualify for one of the threatened categories within five years.

Near threatened: A species that does not qualify for conservation dependent, but is close to qualifying as vulnerable.

Least concern: A species that does not qualify for conservation dependent or near threatened.

Data deficient: A species on which there is inadequate information to make an asssessment of risk of extinction. Because there is a possibility that future research will show that the species is threatened, more information is required.

The categories from the *IUCN Red List of Threatened Plants*, used in *Endangered Wildlife and Plants of the World*, are as follows:

Extinct: A species that has not definitely been located in the wild during the last 50 years.

Endangered: A species whose survival is unlikely if the factors that threaten it continue. Included are species whose numbers have been reduced to a critical level, or whose habitats have been so drastically reduced that they are deemed to be in immediate danger of extinction. Also included in this category are species that may be extinct but have definitely been seen in the wild in the past 50 years.

Vulnerable: A species that is thought likely to move into the endangered category in the near future if the factors that threaten it remain.

Rare: A species with small world populations that are not at present endangered or vulnerable, but are at risk. These species are usually in restricted areas or are thinly spread over a larger range.

TABLE OF CONTENTS

Volume 2

Volume 3

Volume 4

Volume 6

Volume 7

Volume 8

Volume 9

Volume 11

ABUTILON

Order: Magnoliopsida

Family: Malvaceae

The genus *Abutilon* comprises some 150 distinct species, the majority of which are native to the New World, in tropical and subtropical regions. *Abutilon* is a Greek name for malvaceous plants; the old name for the genus is *Abortopetalum*. The plants discussed are all referred to as flowering maples, a common name that is confusingly applied to several separate species. *Abutilon* species are usually pubescent, perennial herbs or shrubs with simple leaves and white, yellow, orange, or dark red flowers.

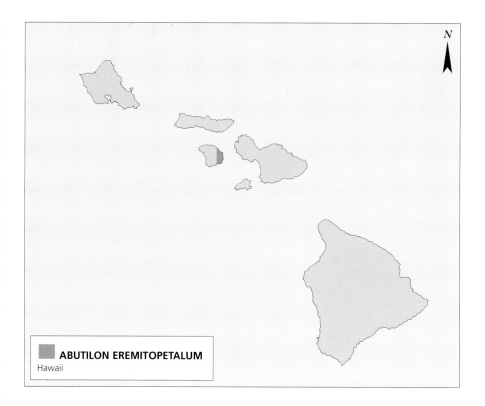

ABUTILON EREMITOPETALUM
Hawaii

Abutilon Eremitopetalum

ESA: Endangered

IUCN: Endangered

Height: Up to 16 in. (41 cm)

Stems: Slightly hairy

Leaves: Cordate to ovate up to 4¾ in. (12 cm) long

Flowers: April to June. Solitary or in pairs, up to 1½ in. (4 cm), generally shades of green with a hint of red

Pollination: By insect

Habitat: Dry forest at heights of up to 1,640 ft. (500 m)

Range: Eastern Lanai, Hawaii

ABUTILON EREMITOPETALUM is also known as *Abutilon cryptopetalum*, although this latter name is now found only in older texts. Some texts now refer to it as the flowering maple. This shrub has been regarded as rare ever since its initial scientific description was published in 1934, although it was first found in the 1920s.

This plant was initially recorded from Kalulu and Maunalei Valley, both in eastern Lanai. For many years these were the only two sites known to support this species, although many similar habitat types were found and checked. Eventually a new population of this plant was discovered in 1987 in the Kehewai Gulch. This latter population is of only 60 to 70 plants.

There is one other site that is of importance for this species, and that is the dry forest of Kanepu'u. At this site naturalized populations have been grown since the 1920s and 1930s. It is strongly felt that further exploration in this area may reveal naturally occurring populations. The plant thus occurs naturally in only three locations, with an overall population of up to 300 individuals.

Near relation

Abutilon eremitopetalum is closely related to the equally rare *Abutilon menziesii*, from which it most noticeably differs in the flower color. *Abutilon eremitopetalum* has green or reddish brown flowers, whereas *Abutilon menziesii* has dark red, white, or yellow flowers. The stamens of the flowering maple protrude from the flower, which is not the case for *Abutilon menziesii*.

Abutilon eremitopetalum has stems with small hairs, and from these stems come the simple leaves, which are generally spade-shaped. Borne in the axils between the leaves and the stems are the single or paired flowers. The leaves are considerably longer than the flowers, so in this species, because of their color, the flowers are often difficult to distinguish at first glance. When

the native flora. Predation from non-native animals is a threat. They will often cause more damage than the native species with which the plant has evolved.

A final threat is the action of humans. As a plant becomes more rare its value correspondingly increases to collectors. As the human population expands, the pressure exerted on the land also increases, and urban development and road building escalate proportionately.

Recovery programs are in operation for *Abutilon eremitopetalum*. It is illegal to collect the plant without a permit. The sites in which this species grow are relatively protected due to their remote location.

There are many examples of suitable habitat around the island of Lanai, and with various growth plans in operation, it is hoped that outplanting of new colonies will aid in the continued survival of this species.

Growth of plants is taking place in the wild—in the Kanepu'u site previously mentioned—as well as at botanical gardens and universities throughout the world.

As with all rare or endangered species, more research will give us more knowledge about this species, which will in turn aid its survival and spread.

The common name of field maple is actually applied to several other members of the genus *Abutilon*. To avoid confusion it is advisable to avoid this common name and always use the scientific name.

the seeds are produced they are rarely as large as 3 millimeters; they are white or brown with a slight pubescence.

Many threats

As with many plants endemic to islands, the threats faced by this species are related most directly to its location, and there is always an additional threat on a volcanic island. A species that is represented by only three known populations, totaling some 200 to 300 wild growing individuals, will always be at risk from any environmental disaster, especially a volcanic eruption.

Another threat is competition with alien species. As people move to an area, they bring non-native plants and animals with them. Because of a lack of natural predators for these non-native species, it is often possible for plants to outcompete

Abutilon Menziesii

ESA: Endangered

IUCN: Endangered

Height: 8 ft. (2.5 m)
Stems: Up to 8 ft. (2.5 m) long
Leaves: Coarsely toothed, silvery, and heart shaped, ¾–2 in. (2–5 cm) long
Flowers: April to June. Red, ¾ in. (2 cm) across
Pollination: By insect
Habitat: Field margins
Range: Maui and Lanai of the Hawaiian Islands

ABUTILON MENZIESII plants, sometimes known locally as Ko' oloa' ula, are found on the margins of fields and at the sides of washed-out gullies, but it is believed that these are the last vestiges of the original distribution of this species.

Because these areas are merely refugia, it is believed that these locations do not represent the true habitat requirements of this species.

The exact habitat requirements are in fact unknown, which makes any recovery plan even more difficult to formulate. This plant was first collected from Hawaii in the early 1790s, at which time it was reported as growing on Hawaii, Lanai, and Maui. At the end of the 20th century, only three populations were known. The largest population is on the island of Maui, and this

Abutilon menziesii has declined largely due to the loss of its habitat to cultivation. Consequently it thrives only in areas where cultivation is impossible.

numbers only 30 individuals. The other two known populations are on Lanai, and between them they equal in number that of the Maui population.

One of the problems encountered by this plant is increased loss of habitat to cultivation. The plant is now viable only in areas where cultivation is not really a possibility. Another problem for the continued survival of *Abutilon*

menziesii is the fact that it bears a resemblance to another member of the same genus, *Abutilon grandifolium*. *Abutilon grandifolium* is regarded as a common weed, and farmers go to great lengths to try to eradicate this viscous plant from their pineapple and sugarcane plantations.

This has probably lead to unrecorded populations of *Abutilon menziesii* being destroyed.

ABUTILON MENZIESII
Hawaii

There are a number of other factors that threaten the continued survival of *Abutilon menziesii*, including its unsuitable habitat. The gullies where some of the plants live are prone to flash floods during the rainy season, and during the summer they are equally prone to drying out. These two extremes of water level place increased stress on *Abutilon menziesii*, much more than if it were exposed to just one of the conditions.

Pests and threats

Grazing pressure from herbivorous animals can also be problematical. This plant is not a favored food source, although it will be eaten by animals when there is little else around.

Grazing pressure was responsible for the demise of the Hawaii population of *Abutilon menziesii* during a year of drought. *Abutilon menziesii* also has a predator species in the form of the Chinese rose beetle (*Adoretus sinicus*). Since the Chinese rose beetle is not native to Hawaii, there are no natural predators to keep its numbers under control, and it is regarded as a major pest species of *Abutilon menziesii* and related plants.

The situation with this plant is so extreme that taking only exceptional steps may save it. All of the known plants are currently found on plantations and farms that are privately owned. One suggestion is to transplant all plants from these areas to the botanical gardens of Hawaii. This is a very extreme measure that may ultimately lead to failure and the extinction of *Abutilon menziesii*. For true and continued survival of the species, it should be left in its natural habitat, but, as has already been stated, the exact original habitat is unknown. The populations that can be seen are all in extremes of habitat, and they are surviving by the narrowest of margins.

If cultivation of this plant were more successful than has been currently proven, then experiments could be carried out to ascertain the best habitat for continued survival.

Once these conditions were known, then appropriate land could be selected on each of the original islands from which the species was known, and these patches of land could be set aside as reserves. This would make continued survival more likely, because the plants would then be spread out over several different areas. With only three known populations of *A. menziesii*, a small natural event could easily eradicate them.

One remaining problem is that with a total population of some 60 individuals, there is a deficit of genetic material. This means the plants are less likely to be able to adapt to any future change in their circumstances, and *Abutilon menziesii* will remain in a perilous situation.

Abutilon Sandwicense

ESA: Endangered

IUCN: Endangered

Height: Generally 5–10 ft. (1.5–3 m) tall, although exceptionally 19½ ft. (6 m) tall
Stems: Yellowish and pubescent
Leaves: Thin and spade-like, 3–10 in. (8–25 cm) long
Flowers: April to June. Bright green to reddish brown and borne close to the stem
Pollination: By insect
Habitat: Steep slopes of dry forest at 985–1,970 ft. (300–600 m) elevation
Range: Between the Makaleha Valley and Pu'ukaua in the Waianae Mountains on the island of Oahu, Hawaii

ABUTILON SANDWICENSE is one of 150 different species of the genus *Abutilon*, many of which are simply referred to as field maples. This species does not have its own common name, and this fact can lead to confusion about exactly which species is being discussed. The scientific name will be used exclusively here. It should be borne in mind that this species has had several previous scientific names that may be encountered in older literature. These names are *Abortopetalum sandwicense* and *Abutilon sandwicense* var. *welchii*. *Abutilon sandwicense* is currently the accepted correct name for this species. The variety *welchii* is now thought merely to be an example of the normal range of character

variation that can be found within this species.

Abutilon sandwicense is one of the larger members of this genus, sometimes attaining a height of 19½ feet (6 meters). The flowers are produced singly in the axils of the leaves and are very pendulous and quite obvious, being up to 4 inches (10 centimeters) long, while individual petals are normally a maximum of 2 inches (5 centimeters).

The whole plant is pubescent, densely in some parts and with stellate hairs on the stem. The many seeds produced are sparsely pubescent and scarcely reach 3 millimeters in length.

The flower color, which is bright green to reddish brown, and size, along with the overall size of the plant, readily distinguish it from the other species of *Abutilon*.

ABUTILON SANDWICENSE
Hawaii

Abutilon sandwicense has always been considered rare and its occurrence in only one region on a small volcanic island makes it a particularly endangered taxon. Any species as confined as this one is can be liable to extinction from just one natural disaster, such as a volcanic eruption.

As with many endemic island species, many of the problems facing its continued survival are related to human activity. The introduction of non-native animals to the island has lead to a depletion of stock due to grazing pressure. An island-growing species will normally be adapted to the animals around it, but new animals may exert pressures to which the plant is unable to react. Goats in particular can reach the habitat of *Abutilon sandwicense*, and they are capable of cropping vegetation very close to the ground, thus killing the plant. Invasive plants can cause similar problems. A non-native plant introduced into an area where it has no natural predators can spread very rapidly, and it may outcompete native plants for resources.

Growth on a limited scale has been successful at several botani-

cal gardens and universities throughout the world. It is hoped that this will lead to an eventual reintroduction of the species into the wild. Ideally, reintroduction will be carried out in areas that are not currently inhabited by *Abutilon sandwicense*. Spreading members of the species over a variety of suitable habitats will strengthen its position and make continued survival more likely. One problem with this approach is that because the species is currently rare, there are few individuals that can be used for breeding. There are only several hundred plants known to occur in the wild. Because the recovery is being carried out from a limited stock, the full variability present within the species may be lost. This can result in a genetic bottleneck that may lead to problems in the future, such as the loss of the ability of the plant to react to any drastic changes in the environment. Also, plants that are genetically related may be incapable of breeding together due to incompatibility of their reproductive mechanisms.

More research is needed on this species to determine its exact growth requirements. Knowing these requirements will allow suitable habitats to be chosen as reserves for outplanting.

The greatest hope for survival of this species is to increase the number of areas in which it is found and to ensure wherever possible that these areas are geographically separated.

Gordon Rutter

Addax

(Addax nasomaculatus)

IUCN: Endangered

Class: Mammalia
Order: Artiodactyla
Family: Bovidae
Weight: 220–300 lb.
(100–140 kg)
Shoulder height: 39–47 in.
(100–120 cm)
Diet: Grass, leaves, twigs
Gestation period: 250–265
days
Longevity: 15–20 years
Habitat: Desert
Range: Sahara, north Africa

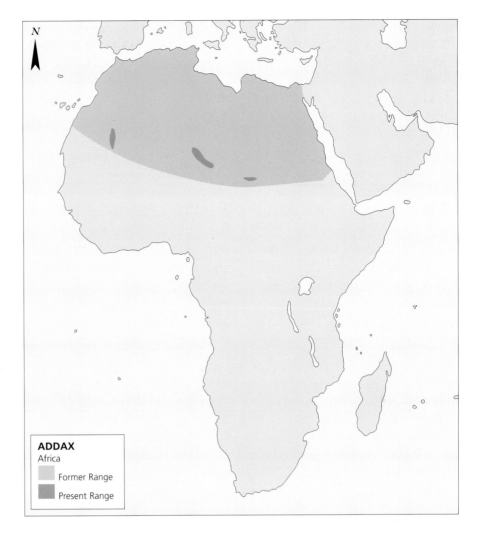

ADDAX
Africa
Former Range
Present Range

THE ADDAX IS a true desert animal. It is supremely adapted to survive in some of the world's most hostile environments. Its short white coat gives some insulation and reflects the penetrating desert sun. Of all antelope, it has the broadest hooves in proportion to its size. This allows it to move quickly and surefootedly over shifting sand and gravel. It has the ability to survive for long periods without drinking water, deriving moisture from the vegetation it eats. This vegetation is sparse, so the addax must spend most of its waking hours foraging to find enough food to sustain itself.

Spiral horns

Both sexes possess long, spiraling horns. The adults of both sexes can be identified from a distance by the number of spirals. Females generally have two open spirals, while males exhibit three. Female horns also tend to be longer than the male's, but the male's horns are thicker. Other than these differences, the sexes differ very little in either size or general appearance. Addax may reach a height of 47 inches (120 centimeters) at the shoulder and live for as long as 20 years.

In summer this species' coat is all white, changing to a buff tan in winter. There is a patch of long hair that is roughly circular on the forehead and between the horns, which gives the addax the appearance of wearing a toupee. This hair remains a uniform brown color throughout the year.

The nomadic life

Solitary male addax are occasionally encountered in nature, but most addax are found in small family groups of four to six. Sometimes these groups are even larger. Because they are nomadic, conflicts between individuals occur more commonly over dominance rather than over territory—territory has less significance when a species has no single home.

Increased hunting

In the wild, the addax faces few predators because very few predators can exist in such a demanding environment. The addax would still be numerous if humans had not encroached upon this environment and if they had not developed more efficient hunting skills. For centuries humans hunted addax from the backs of camels and horses, and the number of addax that were killed was negligible. However, the 20th century brought motorized vehicles capable of moving people and their animals into the addax's range more often and with devastating effect. This encroachment, combined with modern weapons such as rifles, has endangered the addax species. Its range, which used to encompass most of the Sahara region, is now reduced to small scattered areas in Chad, Niger, Mauritania, Sudan, and Mali. The future of these wild populations is in great jeopardy.

Reintroduced

Captive populations, however, offer some hope for the survival of this species. Following World War II, a number of addax were imported to zoos in North America and Europe. This resulted in the establishment of what appear to be healthy, self-sustaining captive populations. These captive populations act as a reservoir from which addax may be reintroduced into the wild. Small numbers have now been reintroduced into fenced enclosures in Tunisia and Morocco. The Tunisian population has increased to approximately 50 individuals.

Unfortunately, the captive population of more than 2,000 animals is based on a very limited gene pool of less than ten individuals. Without more animals to diversify the breeding, the health of this population cannot be guaranteed.

Warren D. Thomas

During the heat of the day, addax spend a lot of time resting. They are active mostly at dawn and dusk and during the cool desert night.

AKEPAS

Class: Aves
Order: Passeriformes
Family: Drepanididae
Subfamily: Psittirostrinae

Akepas are one of several species of birds that are known as honeycreepers. They inhabit native forests on the four Hawaiian islands of Hawaii, Kauai, Maui, and Oahu. Each island's population is considered a separate race or subspecies. The Oahu race may be extinct, and a few ornithologists believe that the Kauai akepa may be a distinct species because of differences in vocal sounds and nesting preferences. The Kauai akepa nests on branches, while all others nest in tree cavities.

The akepa's arboreal lifestyle may have been the factor that saved it. Because the akepa spends nearly all of its time in the canopy formed by the interlocking crowns of trees, it is not so vulnerable to ground-dwelling predators such as house cats (*Felis sylvestris*), Polynesian rats (*Rattus exulans*), Norway rats (*R. norvegicus*), black rats (*R. rattus*), and Indian mongooses (*Herpestes auropunctatus*).

Primarily insectivorous, the akepa depends on a special tool for catching its prey. Its beak crosses very slightly at the tip, apparently helping the akepa open buds to find and extract hidden insects. This distinctive feature represents only one of many special beak adaptations among the honeycreepers.

Hawaii Akepa

(Loxops coccineus coccineus)

ESA: Endangered

IUCN: Endangered

Length: 4–5 in. (10–13 cm)
Weight: ⅓ oz. (9 g)
Clutch size: Unknown
Incubation: Unknown
Diet: Mostly insects, spiders, and occasionally nectar
Habitat: Natural forests of ohia and koa trees
Range: Limited to eastern Mauna Kea, eastern and southern Mauna Loa, and northern Hualalai on the island of Hawaii

AKEPAS ONCE LIVED abundantly in the lush natural forests of the island of Hawaii. Today they are one of eight species of Hawaiian forest birds considered to be endangered.

The male Hawaii akepa is bright red orange, with brownish wings and tail; the female is gray green with a yellow breast. The Hawaii akepa population has declined as the island's forests have deteriorated. This bird prefers the dense canopy formed by the interlocking crowns of koa (*Acacia koa*) and ohia (*Metrosideros collina*) trees. It has been seen in mamane trees (*Sophora chrysophylla*) as well, but this tree does not appear to be its preferred habitat. In the canopy, the Hawaii akepa works patiently, twig by twig, gleaning caterpillars and spiders from crevices and buds. The Hawaii akepa also breeds in the trees, where it is known to use abandoned cavities to build its nest. Very little study has been done on this bird's reproductive cycle, and only three nests have ever been found. Details of courtship, nest building, and rearing of young are not known.

Once people settled on Hawaii, the Hawaii akepa faced unfamiliar dangers, for which it had no defense strategies. The earliest Hawaiians valued the male's bright plumage, and countless birds were killed to provide feathered skins for robes and other finery. People also brought new plants and animals to the islands with them. Some of

Like many endangered species, the Hawaii akepa's population has declined severely due to deforestation.

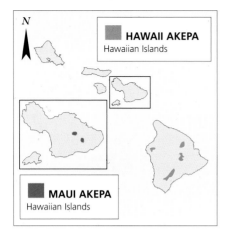

HAWAII AKEPA
Hawaiian Islands

MAUI AKEPA
Hawaiian Islands

these animals carried avian disease, some of the animals preyed on or competed with the akepas, and others degraded the forests where the akepas lived. Native forests were cut for firewood and building materials, and later cleared for farming and cattle grazing. Exotic plant growth also harmed the akepa's habitat. All of these factors operated simultaneously to endanger the akepas, and as the forests gradually dwindled away, the Hawaii akepa dwindled with them.

A survey in 1976 estimated that there were 5,300 akepas in and around the Kau Forest Reserve. No akepas were seen in Volcanoes National Park, although they were reported to have been seen in that area during the 1940s.

The Hawaii Forest Bird Recovery Plan was completed in 1982. A cooperative venture of the U.S. Fish and Wildlife Service, National Park Service, Forest Service, Hawaii Division of Forestry, and the University of Hawaii, the plan aimed to increase the population level enough to justify removing the species from endangered status. Many specific tasks were identified in the plan, but certain objectives stood out.

The plan recommended that, first, the remaining natural forests of koa and ohia had to be protected from further damage. This meant protecting them from exotic plants and animals and from cutting either for lumber or grazing interests. Second, the natural forests had to be regenerated and restored. Third, captive breeding needed to be explored. And fourth, the akepa's basic natural history needed to be more completely understood.

In 1985 the Hakalau Forest National Wildlife Reserve was created to protect Hawaii's forest birds. This area contains a great diversity of native flora and fauna, including eight endangered bird species, one of which is the Hawaii akepa. Current surveys estimate that there are now around 14,000 Hawaii akepas in three separate populations.

When the first Polynesians arrived on Hawaii in the first millennium C.E., they found a spectacle of seabirds and unique landbirds living on the islands. Discounting the seabirds, they still found almost 90 species. By the time James Cook opened the Hawaiian Islands to the world in 1778, the Polynesians had exterminated 39 bird species, including 2 ibises, 7 geese, a hawk, an eagle, 3 owls, 7 rails, and 18 songbirds. At least 14 more species, including 2 rails and 12 songbirds, have become extinct since Cook's day, and another dozen species are precariously close to extinction.

The Hawaii akepa is not as critically endangered as some Hawaiian birds but its numbers are still considered low enough for it to remain on the list of endangered species.

Maui Akepa
(Loxops coccineus ochraceus)

ESA: Endangered

IUCN: Endangered

Length: 4–5 in. (10–13 cm)
Weight: ⅓ oz. (9 g)
Clutch size: Unknown
Incubation: Unknown
Diet: Insects and spiders
Habitat: Ohia and koa trees
Range: Forests at 2,000–7,000 ft. (610–2,135 m) elevation on the north side of Haleakala Crater, Maui, Hawaiian Islands

THE MAUI AKEPA may be the rarest of the akepas. It was seen only six times in the 20th century, before 1980, when eight birds were found. Local experts suspect that approximately 230 birds may still be alive.

The male Maui akepa is orange or yellow; females are gray green with yellow breasts; the beak of both sexes is gray. Preferring the native ohia (*Metrosideros collina*) tree, the Maui akepa looks for insects in the outer leaves and twigs. It occasionally takes nectar from ohia blossoms. Both koa and ohia trees are essential to the bird, and protection plans focus on preserving native forests. Essential steps include controlling pigs, goats, cattle, and axis deer that damage the trees. The spread of exotic plants can also harm native plants and prevent natural reforestation. Education and research about the Maui akepa's natural history are also important to the recovery of this species.

Kevin Cook

AKIALOAS

Class: Aves

Order: Passeriformes

Family: Drepanididae

Subfamily: Psittirostrinae

Akialoas are one of several species commonly called Hawaiian honeycreepers. Like other birds known by this name, akialoas creep about tree trunks and large branches, where they search for their prey.

Some observers in the last century wrote about seeing akialoas pecking at bark in much the same way as a woodpecker, although not as forcefully. These birds use their long, curved beaks to probe into bark crevices, behind mosses and lichens, and into holes, from which they extract invertebrates. Caterpillars, beetles, weevils, crickets, and cockroaches comprise much of their diet, although more than one observer has commented on the akialoa's particular fondness for spiders. Occasionally akialoas will take nectar from ohia and lobelia blossoms.

One study of Hawaiian birds speculated that akialoas sing more frequently when they feed on nectar. If this is true, it is possible that nectar feeding is somehow associated with breeding, because singing is often related to the bird's defensive territorial behavior and mating habits.

While foraging, akialoas work the trees from ground level to the crown, but observers have also seen the Kauai akialoa probing among forest litter on the ground. If such feeding behavior is common, it may be contributing to this bird's disappearance, because it makes them more vulnerable to predators. The akialoas are just one more of the Hawaiian forest bird groups that is rapidly disappearing. Unlike birds that live on continents, island species are hopelessly isolated, unable to move to better, stable habitats and escape the destruction of their old range. Unless humans begin taking measures to preserve their habitat, there is little hope for these birds.

Akialoa

(Hemignathus obscurus)

IUCN: Extinct

Length: 6½–7 in. (17–18 cm); beak often 2 in. (5 cm) or longer, the male's beak was longer than that of the female

Weight: Unknown

Clutch size: Unknown

Incubation: Unknown

Diet: Primarily insects and spiders, but also nectar

Habitat: Dense native forests of ohia and koa, possibly above 2,000 ft. (610 m) elevation

Range: Hawaii, Lanai, and Oahu in the Hawaiian Islands

THE AKIALOA WAS bright yellow and green on the upperparts of its body, while its underparts were a golden greenish yellow. The lores were black, and the beak was long, thin, and sickle-shaped.

The akialoa once inhabited dense native forests on the islands of Hawaii, Lanai, and Oahu. The Oahu subspecies (*Hemignathus obscurus ellisianus*) has not been seen since it was last collected in 1837. Few written records document the Lanai subspecies (*Hemignathus obscurus lanaiensis*), and ornithologists consider it to be, likewise, extinct in the last century.

Survival hope

The Hawaii subspecies of the akialoa (*Hemignathus obscurus obscurus*) survived longer, and was described as plentiful in the 1890s. But its demise was swift, and all observations that were recorded after the first decade of the 20th century are therefore suspect. However, other Hawaiian birds have been considered extinct, then rediscovered again decades later. There is a faint possibility that the akialoa still survives in a dense ohia forest on the islands of Hawaii.

Kauai Akialoa

(Hemignathus procerus)

ESA: Endangered

Length: 7–7½ in. (18–19 cm); beak often 2 in. (5 cm) or longer, the male's beak is longer than that of the female

Weight: Unknown

Clutch size: Unknown

Incubation: Unknown

Diet: Primarily insects and spiders, but also nectar

Habitat: Native forests of ohia and koa

Range: Kauai, Hawaiian Islands

SOME ORNITHOLOGISTS regard the Kauai akialoa as a subspecies of the *Hemignathus* genus rather than a separate species. If this is so, the birds of Kauai, Lanai, and Oahu would be subspecies of *Hemignathus ellisianus*, and the Hawaii akialoa would be a dis-

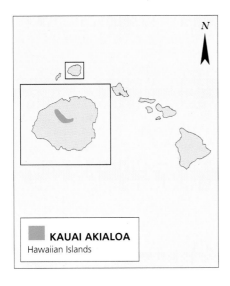

KAUAI AKIALOA
Hawaiian Islands

tinct separate species called *Hemignathus obscurus.*

In males, the coloration is a yellowish olive green above and golden greenish yellow below; females are grayer above. Both sexes have black lores and long, sickle-shaped beaks.

The Kauai akialoa was considered rare, but was more common than other native forest birds into the closing decades of the 19th century. Kauai akialoas were seen and collected in 1900. By the middle of the 20th century, however, most ornithologists believed they were extinct. But then two were found in 1960 in Kauai's Alakai Swamp; the species was last seen in 1965. After so many years' absence, it seems unlikely that this bird will be seen much in the 21st century.

Recovery

It is difficult to protect a species that may be extinct. Another hindrance is that virtually nothing is known of its natural history. As of 1983, the Kauai Forest Bird Recovery Plan—cooperatively produced by the U.S. Fish and Wildlife Service and the Hawaii Division of Forestry—targeted several actions to possibly preserve the species. Most of them relate to maintaining or improving habitat quality by protecting the remaining native forests, controlling grazing by livestock and feral animals, and controlling predation by mammals.

Kevin Cook

Akiapolaau

(Hemignathus wilsoni)

ESA: Endangered

IUCN: Endangered

Class: Aves
Order: Passeriformes
Family: Drepanididae
Subfamily: Psittirostrinae
Length: 5½–6 in. (14–15 cm)
Weight: 1 oz. (28 g)
Clutch size: Unknown
Incubation: Unknown
Diet: Primarily insects and spiders, but also nectar
Habitat: Native koa forests
Range: Fragmented populations on the island of Hawaii in the Hawaiian Islands at elevations above 1,300 ft. (400 m)

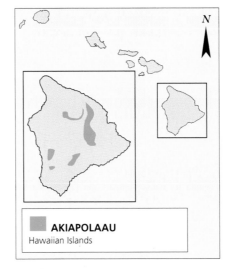

AKIAPOLAAU
Hawaiian Islands

of a nuthatch. The akiapolaau works the trunks and larger branches of trees. It hammers the bark with the short lower half of its beak, then probes with the long, thin, pointed upper half of the beak to pry out and capture beetle larvae and insects.

The head and underparts of the akiapolaau are bright yellow; the wings and upperparts are olive green. As is the case with many birds, the females are a duller color. There is a black ring

THE BEHAVIOR of an akiapolaau is like that of a woodpecker, but its stocky physique is more like that

circling the eyes, which are set in a rather large head. The tail is short, giving the bird a chunky appearance.

Population

Despite being reported as a rather common species, even into the middle decades of the 20th century, the akiapolaau remains as little known as other, rarer species. Only two nests have been found, and both were abandoned before they were completed. This species, now numbering perhaps 1,500, has presumably declined because of the same problems that have affected other Hawaiian honeycreepers. Much native forest land has been destroyed for timber production or agriculture, and especially for livestock grazing at higher elevations. The akiapolaau suffers from habitat loss more easily than other species because its range is restricted to the island of Hawaii.

Forest degradation began with the arrival of the first Polynesian

The akiapolaau is severely affected by habitat loss due to its already limited range on the Hawaiian Islands. Any minor loss is a huge setback.

settlers and accelerated in the early 1800s. The quality of the remaining forest has been severely compromised by the introduction of exotic plants and grazing mammals such as pigs, cattle, goats, sheep, and deer.

A team of biologists from the U.S. Fish and Wildlife Service, the Hawaii Division of Forestry, the U.S. Forest and National Park Services, and the University of Hawaii devised the Hawaii Forest Bird Recovery Plan in 1982. The mission of the plan is to stabilize, and even boost, populations of birds such as the akiapolaau to a nonendangered status. The plan calls for protecting remaining native forests and controlling the factors that threaten their quality.

This bird is found in the Hakalau Forest National Wildlife Reserve, which was created in 1985 to protect Hawaii's forest birds. It is also found in the recently created Kona Forest Unit within the Hakalau reserve. The Kona Forest Unit contains native forest dominated by koa an ohia trees. This provides an ideal protected habitat for the akiapolaau.

Kevin Cook

Ala Balik

(Salmo platycephalus)

ESA: Endangered

IUCN: Critically endangered

Class: Actinopterygii
Order: Salmoniformes
Family: Salmonidae
Length: 16 in. (40 cm)
Reproduction: Egg layer
Habitat: Stream pools and rapids
Range: Seyhan River basin, Turkey

RESTRICTED TO A few small segments of the upper reaches of eastern Turkey's Seyhan River and its tributaries, the ala balik is considered to be a rare fish. Only a few specimens have ever been found in this mountainous area of Turkey, which is near the small town of Pinarbasi. Neighboring river drainages contain fish similar to the ala balik, such as the brown trout (*Salmo trutta*), but the ala balik has not been found to inhabit those streams. This fish seeks the cooler waters of the Seyhan River, which flow from natural springs. The ala balik depends on these springs and the meager amounts of runoff for its survival. If these springs were to be diverted from the riverbed for domestic use or for agriculture, the remaining populations of this critically endangered fish could be lost forever. Efforts to preserve the ala balik must include protection of these life-sustaining freshwater springs.

Freshwater fish

The ala balik is a salmonid, so it has many of the same physical and biological features as the salmon and trout of North America. However, unlike many salmonid fishes, it lives all of its life in a freshwater environment. Other fish such as the coho salmon (*Oncorhynchus kisutch*) hatch in rivers and live the first part of their lives in these rivers and associated lakes. After a period of several months, the physiology of these fish changes, allowing them to migrate downstream and enter the saltwater of the sea. For several years these fish roam the ocean, growing to sexual maturity. Finally, they migrate back to the precise location from which they came in order to spawn. Pacific Ocean salmon die after they spawn, but Atlantic Ocean salmon survive and return to spawn each year. While closely related to the brown trout and Atlantic salmon (*Salmo salar*), the ala balik does not move downstream and enter the Mediterranean Sea to feed. The waters of the sea, and even the lower reaches of the Seyhan River, are too warm for this cold-water fish to survive. Air temperatures in the coastal region commonly climb to over 100 degrees Fahrenheit (38 degrees Centigrade). The ala balik is trapped in the Seyhan River, with no opportunity to expand its range.

Characteristics

The ala balik's streamlined body and strong tail help move it up and down the river to spawn and to chase down prey. It consumes primarily small bottom-dwelling animals—called amphipods—and insects, but may also eat fish if they are available.

As with all salmon and trout, the ala balik has a small, fleshy second dorsal fin called the adipose fin. A unique feature of the ala balik is that while it does have spots and other markings as a juvenile, it has no distinctive markings on its body as an adult. This trait is unusual in salmonids and, along with its bright yellow-orange fins, is a useful means of identification. Its species name, *platycephalus*, means "flat head," which aptly describes the broad and flat shape of its head. The ala balik has large eyes and feeds primarily by sight. Little else is known about the ala balik. If it behaves as other salmonids do, it probably spawns in the fall.

William E. Manci

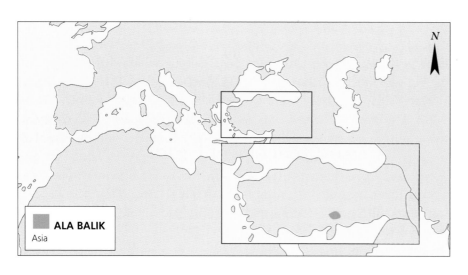

ALA BALIK
Asia

N

ALBATROSSES

Class: Aves

Order: Procellariiformes

Family: Diomedeidae

Albatrosses command the sea and sky in a way unequaled by any other bird. Although they swim well on the surface, they do not dive. Their talent lies in soaring flight. Albatross bones are more completely hollow than the bones of any other bird. This attribute makes them comparatively light for their size and, therefore, more buoyant in flight. Their long, narrow wings possess more flight feathers (up to 50) than the wings of other birds. Such wing structure allows the albatross to sail with little flapping on the complex air currents that develop over the swells, troughs, and waves of the open sea.

Albatrosses are pelagic, which means they live over the open sea and seldom visit land. They go ashore only for nesting, leaving them no access to fresh water. In common with other birds, they swallow seawater as they feed and balance the body's salt intake with special glands located between the eyes and the base of the beak. These glands remove excess salt from their blood and eliminate it as a clear fluid through tubular nostrils. This is a characteristic of the order (Procellariiformes) to which albatrosses belong.

Albatrosses have an unusual breeding cycle. They lay a single egg, which requires more than two months to incubate. The parent birds take turns brooding the chick for another month or so. When one parent can no longer keep the growing chick fed, both parents leave the chick unguarded as they forage at sea. They return at irregular intervals to feed the chick, which requires another five to six months before it becomes a fledgling. Immature birds may wander at sea for as few as two or as many as nine years before returning to the islands where they were raised.

Once mated, albatrosses remain paired for life. They do form new pairs if a mate is lost, but separations between living mates are exceptionally rare. All the albatross species perform elaborate rituals of bowing and beak clapping, which help mates recognize each other and keep pair bonds strong even after long absences.

Because each breeding season lasts so long, albatrosses ordinarily breed only every other year. If an egg or chick is lost early enough in a given season, the pair will abandon the effort for that year and then attempt to breed again the following season. Albatrosses have an average life span of 40 years.

Amsterdam Island Albatross

(Diomedea amsterdamensis)

ESA: Endangered

IUCN: Critically endangered

Length: Unknown, but probably 3–4 ft. (0.9–1.2 m)

Weight: Average 13–14 lb. (6–6.4 kg)

Clutch size: 1 egg

Incubation: 76–83 days

Diet: Unknown

Habitat: Open ocean; breeds only on Amsterdam Island in the southern Indian Ocean

Range: Distribution at sea after breeding not known, but presumed to be Indian Ocean

THE AMSTERDAM ISLAND albatross escaped detection until 1979. It was first described as a species in 1983, but not all ornithologists yet accept the bird as a distinct species. In many respects, it closely resembles the wandering albatross (*Diomedea exulans*), which is a diverse species with several color variations. The Amsterdam Island albatross differs in being slightly smaller, having a dark beak tip and mouth stripe, a white eyelid rather than blue, and showing an overall darker plumage. These are minor differences of appearance; however, the most important difference is behavioral. The Amsterdam Island albatross begins laying in late February, almost two months later than the wandering albatross and nearly three months later than the royal albatross (*D. epomophora*). Subtle physical differences can be easily explained as geographic variation within a given species, but breeding differences cannot.

The Amsterdam Island albatross breeds farther north than any known population of wandering albatross. Although wandering albatrosses regularly visit the waters around Amsterdam Island, none has ever been known to breed there. The albatrosses of Amsterdam Island have higher-pitched voices than those of wandering albatrosses. They also display some differences in courtship rituals. The physical isolation of the island, the delayed onset of the breeding season for the island's only albatrosses, and variations in courtship rituals argue that the birds are reproductively isolated and therefore qualify as a separate species.

Amsterdam Island is only 22 square miles (57 square kilometers), with steep cliffs on the southwest rising to 2,300 feet (700 meters). The island slopes gently downward to the northeast. The Amsterdam Island albatrosses nest inland on the northern slope about 1,500 to 2,100 feet (about 460 to 640 meters) above the sea. Mosses, ferns, clubmosses, grasses, and sedges grow around the nesting site. Recovered bones indicate that albatrosses once bred over much of the northern expanse of the island. Presumably, the scattered bones mean that the breeding population was once much larger than at present. In 1978 five fledglings were recorded, indicating at least five breeding pairs. Only one pair was observed nesting in 1981. In 1987 this number had risen to twelve pairs and a total of 11 pairs were observed in 1988. Because the species breeds every other year, it is probable that two dozen breeding pairs plus several unmated, nonbreeding individuals exist, bringing the total population to about 65 birds.

Threats from people

Since its discovery in 1522, Amsterdam Island has been visited regularly by explorers, whalers, sealers, and fishers. The unwary albatrosses have made easy prey for hungry sea travelers. People also brought rats, cats, dogs, pigs, and cattle to the island. Although the dogs and pigs have died out, the cats, rats, and cattle remain. Some naturalists question whether cats and rats are large enough to be significant predators of albatross eggs and chicks. However, feral cattle heavily graze the island, causing degradation of albatross nesting habitat.

The researchers who discovered the Amsterdam Island albatross have suggested erecting fences to exclude cattle from the birds' nesting habitat. Fences, however, are unnatural obstacles which may prove as lethal to the birds as other human actions. A more thorough solution, which would also benefit the island's native plant life, would be to relocate the feral cattle entirely.

Short-Tailed Albatross
(Diomedea albatrus)

ESA: Endangered
IUCN: Endangered

Length: 36 in. (91 cm)
Weight: Unknown
Clutch size: 1 egg
Incubation: 64–65 days
Diet: Mostly squid, crustaceans, and fish, but also known to take offal from whaling ships and galley garbage discarded overboard
Habitat: Open ocean but does wander into coastal waters; comes ashore only to nest
Range: Pacific Ocean, mostly north of the Tropic of Cancer, from North America to Asia, including the Bering Sea and the Sea of Okhotsk

AFTER ENDURING FIVE decades of intense feather collecting, surviving World War II, and withstanding two volcanic eruptions, the short-tailed albatross defeated extinction, even when some ornithologists believed its extinction was certain.

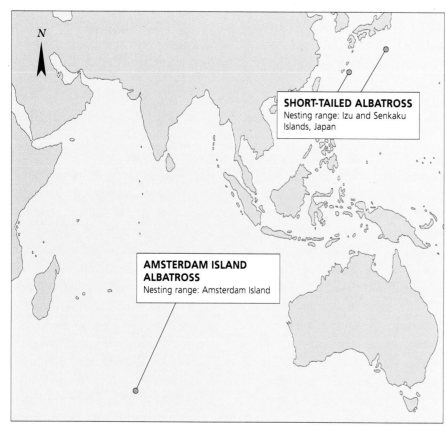

SHORT-TAILED ALBATROSS
Nesting range: Izu and Senkaku Islands, Japan

AMSTERDAM ISLAND ALBATROSS
Nesting range: Amsterdam Island

The short-tailed albatross once ranged widely over the North Pacific. Unlike other albatrosses, it regularly navigated coastal waters, where peoples on both sides of the Pacific captured it for food.

Japanese feather collectors began hunting the albatrosses on Torishima in the Izu Islands in the 1880s. People settled on the island permanently in 1887. Within the next 20 years, 5 million short-tailed albatrosses were killed for their feathers.

Volcanic destruction

A volcano erupted on Torishima in 1902 and buried much of the albatrosses' nesting habitat with lava and ash. By 1929, fewer than 2,000 short-tailed albatrosses survived, and four years later there were fewer than 50. Another volcanic eruption occurred in 1939, causing more nesting habitat to be lost. Sightings dwindled steadily through the 1940s until the species was presumed to be extinct in 1949.

A small population of about 50 birds was found on Torishima in 1951. The population has grown steadily since then. As of 1991, the Torishima population numbered about 500 individuals and was increasing at about 7 percent each year.

The short-tailed albatross has also recovered elsewhere. In 1971 it was found on Minaimikojima in the Senkaku Islands, where birds were occupying 500-foot-high (150-meter-high) cliffs.

The albatross is exquisitely adapted to flight, with bones that are more completely hollow than those of any other bird. This makes the bird comparatively light for its size and more buoyant in flight.

Observation was exceedingly difficult. A Japanese researcher found seven chicks in 1988 and ten in 1991, and estimated the population on this island to consist of about 75 birds, 30 of which were breeding.

Protection efforts

Protection of the short-tailed albatross began in 1933 when the Japanese government designated Torishima as a no-hunting area. The Japanese named Torishima a national monument in 1958, then designated the species itself as a national monument in 1962. The International Council for Bird Preservation cited the short-tailed albatross as endangered in 1960, a status that the U.S. Fish and Wildlife Service acknowledged in June 1970. Studies conducted by the Japanese began in 1976, but active recovery work did not start until 1981. That

work aimed at stabilizing soil against erosion by planting grass in nesting areas. Before the program, breeding for the short-tailed albatross had a success rate of barely 59 percent at best. As the nesting habitat has steadily improved, breeding success has risen to as high as 70 percent. Banding research on Torishima clearly indicates that the short-tailed albatross first breeds at five years of age and, unlike larger albatrosses, probably breeds every year. With adult mortality as low as 5 percent a year and a life span of 40 or more years, the species has the natural capacity to recover. Furthermore, the albatross' habit of wandering at sea for several years probably saved the short-tailed species by placing the last few dozen birds beyond the reach of feather hunters.

Kevin Cook

Alerce

(Fitzroya cupressoides)

ESA: Threatened

IUCN: Rare

Class: Pinopsida
Family: Cupressaceae
Height: Up to 165 ft. (50 m) tall
Trunk: Up to 16 ft. (5 m) in diameter
Leaves: Green to grayish-green
Fruits and seeds: Male and female cones
Flowering season: Cones mature in late spring to early summer, most seed is shed in April to May
Pollination/germination: Wind pollinated
Habitat: Poorly drained lowland areas and in mountains at altitudes of 2,300–3,280 ft. (700–1,000 m)
Range: Southern Chile and adjacent regions of southern Argentina

THE ALERCE, also known as the Patagonian cypress, is one of the largest and oldest living organisms on earth. In fact, the oldest known tree is over 3,600 years old. The trunk is covered with brownish red deeply furrowed, fibrous bark and may be bare of branches for up to 66 feet (20 meters) in older specimens. The leaves are of two types depending on age and they are arranged in alternating whorls of three, rarely two or four, leaves. Juvenile leaves are like the petals of a flower, hooked in profile and flattened, to around 8 millimeters long, whereas on mature branches the leaves are scalelike,

egg-shaped, and overlapping. They are 2.5–3 millimeters long. The fruits of the alerce are male and female cones, which are yellowish white, cylindrical, and slightly tapering at the apex. They are 6 to 8 millimeters long and are predominantly borne at the branchlet tips. Each of the 19 or so scales that make up each cone carry two to six irregular pollen sacs. The female cones are borne at the ends of short lateral shoots. They are of a similar length to the male but differ in color, being at first green, then becoming brown at maturity. They consist of six to nine woody pointed scales, in alternating whorls of three, of which only the upper and middle are fertile. When ripe, the scales gape wide to release the seeds. The seeds have two wings each and are about 8 millimeters in diameter.

Pollination is carried out by wind dispersal. Seedlings grow from four to eight winged seeds (cotyledons) and soon produce juvenile foliage. Initial growth is slow, but under ideal conditions the plants can achieve a height of 3 feet (1 meter) in four years.

Highly prized

The timber of the alerce is highly prized because it is extremely durable and unusually resistant to fungal and insect attack. Logs buried for at least 2,000 years have still been in good enough condition to provide suitable wood for sawn timber. Logging began in the 16th century and reached a peak in the mid-19th century, when overexploitation was at the most devastating level ever recorded in South America. The bleak evidence for this can still be seen: Barren landscapes,

The huge scale of the Alerce (*Fitzroya cupressoides*) is clearly demonstrated here. Excessive logging has hastened the decline of this rare species.

punctuated by the persistent stumps of the giant trees, are all that remain of the spectacular groves that existed during the 20th century.

The alerce is classified as endangered by the IUCN–The World Conservation Union, and is listed on Appendix 1 of the Convention on International Trade in Endangered Species of Wild Fauna and Flora (CITES). It is also listed as threatened in the endangered species act of the U.S.; under this act the importa-

tion of its timber is prohibited. Logging has been banned in Argentina since 1973 and in Chile since 1976. In 1977 the Chilean government declared every living tree a National Monument and made harvesting illegal, but illegal logging in remote areas has been impossible Of greater concern, regeneration from seed is very poor.

Present estimates suggest that the remaining stands of this mighty tree occupy less than 50,000 acres (20,000 hectares), which is only 15 percent of the area once occupied. Molecular evidence suggests that the Argentinian populations, now situated at the head of glaciated valleys close to the Chilean border, represent survivors of small populations that existed east of the Andes, rather than to the west as previously suspected.

Propagation program

Of all the South American conifers, the alerce is perhaps the most highly researched, especially concerning its ecology and conservation. Since 1990 it has been the subject of a propagation program at the Universidad Austral in Valdivia, a Darwin Initiative–funded project aimed at restoring the natural forests of the Chilean Central Depression. It is also part of a major Conifer Conservation Program at the Royal Botanic Gardens in Edinburgh, United Kingdom.

The method of propagation used in Edinburgh is cuttings, because the species rarely forms good seed in the British Isles, due to lack of male cones. Although still a rare tree, cultivation, which is largely restricted to botanic gardens and specialist collections, helps to maintain a more representative and diverse genetic stock.

Fred Rumsey

Cholo Alethe

(Alethe choloensis)

ESA: Endangered

IUCN: Vulnerable

Class: Aves
Order: Passeriformes
Family: Muscicapidae
Subfamily: Turdinae
Length: Unknown
Weight: Unknown
Clutch size: 3 eggs (from single documented nest)
Incubation: Unknown
Diet: Ants and beetles
Habitat: Montane evergreen forests
Range: Thyolo Mountains east of the Shire Valley in southern Malawi and northwest Mozambique, Africa

AS A BIRD OF MONTANE evergreen forests, the Cholo alethe occupies a dwindling habitat that represents the way Africa used to be. These montane forests are evergreen: the trees retain their leaves for more than one growing season. They are called montane because they occur at higher elevations on mountains. Cooler temperatures at higher altitudes affect the kinds of plants that grow there. In montane evergreen forests, trees grow close together, and their crowns interlock to form a continuous canopy 30 to 60 feet (9 to 18 meters)

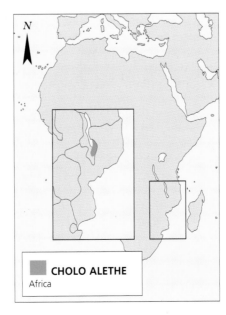

CHOLO ALETHE
Africa

above the ground. This canopy blocks the sun, so very little light reaches the forest floor. Without much light, few smaller plants grow beneath the trees, although some plants such as ferns, mosses, and orchids grow by clinging to the trees themselves.

Scientists have learned that 20,000 years ago the African continent was about 40 degrees cooler than it is today. This was caused by the cooling effect of glaciers in the Northern Hemisphere. As these glaciers melted away, the African continent warmed. This caused the montane forests to gradually shrink. The only evergreen forests left in Africa today are small scattered montane patches, ranging in size from 2 to 1,000 acres (0.8 to 400 hectares).

The populations of animals dependent on montane evergreen forests dwindled with their habitat. Although Africa's forests disappeared naturally, it was gradual. Today, people have hastened the process. Montane evergreen forests produce very little commercially valuable lumber, but people have still cut the forests for firewood and cleared them for agriculture. Birds have nowhere else to go when their habitat is destroyed.

Natural history

Very little is known about the natural history of the Cholo alethe. Observers report that the bird lives on or near the forest floor. Usually seen alone, small flocks of up to five alethes are occasionally found. They have been seen hopping down from logs or low branches into the midst of a group of red ants, then quickly retreating with much wing flapping and beak clicking. Perhaps the cholo alethe has learned to steal insect prey from the ants. Or perhaps the ants become affixed to the bird's plumage and can be picked off later for a meal.

The coloring of the Cholo alethe has been described as a warm earth brown to a deep wood brown on the upperparts, with buff gray or grayish underparts. The chin and throat are a clean white, and outer tail feathers are white-tipped.

Seven other birds in the genus *Alethe* occupy other parts of Africa, but the Cholo alethe is unique to the border country of southern Malawi and adjoining Mozambique. There, it migrates up and down the Thyolo Mountains, spending April to October at lower elevations, then returning to higher elevations to breed from November to January. It remains in the montane evergreen forests throughout its migrations. Where human activities have destroyed forests at lower elevations, the alethe's migrations have presumably been disrupted. The total population in Malawi is estimated at 1,500 pairs, with the most significant populations in Mulanje and Thyolo. No estimate exists for the population in Mozambique.

Forest preservation

A strategy to preserve the cholo alethe would be to preserve the fragments of montane evergreen forests that remain. One of the best ways to achieve forest preservation is to develop alternative fuel sources and more effective agricultural practices.

Kevin Cook

ALLIGATORS

Class: Reptilia

Order: Crocodylia

Family: Alligatoridae

There are two species of alligators, the American and the Chinese. These nontropical crocodilian reptiles are part of the same order as crocodiles and gharials, and all share a similar appearance. Crocodilians move most efficiently in water, but they are able to function on land as well, sliding on the belly or stepping along with legs extended. Alligators and crocodiles may even manage a gallop for short distances.

Alligators differ from crocodiles in the alignment of the upper and lower teeth. They also have a broad snout in comparison to the crocodile's long, narrow one. The Chinese and American alligators share similar burrowing habits. They dig deep holes or dens, as long as 40 feet (12 meters), and hibernate in them during the dry season. They feed primarily on fish, but will occasionally consume crustaceans, insects, and small vertebrates.

Mating habits of the two species are also similar. Both alligators secrete an odorous fluid that attracts the opposite sex during the mating season. As these reptiles reach maturity, their only true enemies are humans, who have succeeded in reducing the populations of alligators significantly. The Chinese alligator has suffered due to habitat loss, but measures established by the government are helping to protect it. The attempts to save the American alligator have been successful and their numbers in the wild have risen dramatically.

American Alligator

(Alligator mississippiensis)

Length: Average 6–12 ft. (1.8–3.7 m), up to 19 ft. (5.8 m)

Clutch size: 20–70 eggs

Incubation: Around 65 days

Diet: Fish

Habitat: Large marsh-bordered lakes, fresh water, and brackish coastal marshes; also savannas

Range: Southeastern United States, west to the Rio Grande in Texas

THE AMERICAN ALLIGATOR is one of the giants of the crocodilian reptiles. Its fingers and toes are joined by webbing; in other crocodilians, webbing occurs only between the toes. The American alligator was intensely hunted for

its hide for many years, and, as with other members of the order Crocodylia, little was done to regulate this practice. The skins were used to make shoes, belts, and bags. By 1967, alligator populations were so severely depleted that the United States government listed the species as endangered.

The comeback of the American alligator has been a major success story. In 1957, due to excessive hunting, there were only 27,000 alligators remaining in Louisiana; today there are over 300,000. The total population in the United States is now around 800,000, and in 1987 the United

States Fish and Wildlife Service (U.S.F.W.S.) pronounced the animal fully recovered and removed it from the list of endangered species. Commercial use of the alligator's hide is still strictly regulated, although there is a controlled industry in Texas and Louisiana.

State and federal protective measures, including listing under the United States Endangered Species Act, has allowed for a marked recovery. By 1975, substantial populations of alligators were recovered in Louisiana, Texas, and Florida. As the numbers increased, the status of the alligator was moved from endan-

The American alligator often basks in the sun to maintain its body temperature.

gered to threatened in coastal areas of Georgia and South Carolina. In Louisiana, Texas, and Florida, its status was changed to threatened due to similarity of appearance (or T/SA), a classification to protect crocodiles that share a similar appearance with the American alligator. By 1987, it was reclassified as T/SA in the remaining areas of its range. It will likely remain under this classification indefinitely.

Under the T/SA classification, states may conduct commercial hunting seasons of the American alligator. With wise management, overexploitation of the species will no longer be a threat. While each state is responsible for its own management of alligators, federal controls are still permitted to facilitate protection of species with a similar appearance that are still threatened. For example, the American crocodile remains close to extinction, and unmonitored hunting of the American alligator could place the crocodile in jeopardy, simply because hunters may not be able to distinguish between the two reptiles. A tagging system is proposed that will permit law enforcement personnel to distinguish between legally taken alligators and illegally taken crocodiles.

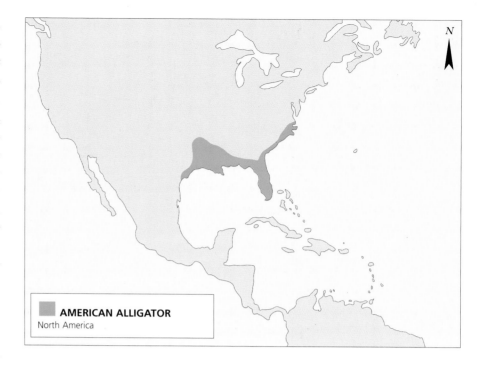

AMERICAN ALLIGATOR
North America

Chinese Alligator
(Alligator sinensis)

ESA: Endangered

IUCN: Critically endangered

Length: Average 4–4½ ft. (1.2–1.4 m), up to 6½ ft. (2 m)
Clutch size: 10–40 eggs
Incubation: 70 days
Diet: Snails, freshwater mussels, fish
Habitat: Lower Yangtze river, adjacent lakes and ponds
Range: People's Republic of China, lower Yangtze valley in Anhui, Zhejiang, and Jiangsu provinces

THE CHINESE ALLIGATOR is a critically endangered species that exists only in the People's Republic of China. The largest population is believed to consist of 300 individuals living in Anhui province. The species has continued to decline in recent years and may even face extinction in the near future.

This species is a relatively small crocodilian, particularly in comparison to the American alligator. The Chinese alligator inhabits low beaches and spends much of its life in burrows excavated in the banks of rivers and ponds. It tends to hibernate from late October until late March or early April. The animals may occasionally leave their burrows on clear days, but they are rather lethargic, moving slowly and rarely vocalizing. During the coldest time of the hibernation period the alligators go into a

Alligators have been portrayed in the media as hostile to people. Consequently they are feared, when in fact they have reason to be wary of humans.

state of deep torpor, neither eating nor moving, and their respiration is greatly reduced. As temperatures increase in late April, the alligators emerge from their caves with increasing frequency, and by early May they are quite active during the day.

By June, as the weather grows hot, the Chinese alligator becomes more nocturnal in its habits. At the same time, the mating season begins. After mating, the female selects a nest site in a concealed area facing the sun and close to water. She uses her forelegs and snout to clear a small area and begins to build a nest of dried leaves and grasses. She lays approximately 10 to 40 eggs in the nest, then adds more leaves and shapes the nest into a mound. Incubation takes about 70 days, and most of the eggs seem to hatch successfully. The new offspring are black with yellow stripes, about 8 inches (20 centimeters) long, and quite agile. The female does not aggressively guard her young after birth, probably because of the large number of young alligators that hatch. They are therefore subject to a wide variety of predators, including turtles, birds, and adults of their own species. Sexual maturity is reached after four or five years, and the Chinese alligator may live to be more than 50 years old.

The Chinese alligator is endemic to the People's Republic of China. This relatively small member of the Crocodylia order is elusive, and, with so few remaining, it is very difficult to study its biology.

This reptile is not as highly prized for its hide as other crocodilians, including the American alligator, but hide hunting has played a role in its decline. Certainly, there have been greater threats. As the human population of China has increased, people have put ever-increasing pressure on the populations of much of the country's wildlife. The Chinese alligator is no exception. As more people utilize the environment, the alligator loses more of its habitat. In addition, alligators residing in grassy bank areas are subjected to flooding, and many drown in their caves if they are unable to reach the water's surface in time. Drought also contributes to the loss of habitat.

China has opened a number of sanctuaries for the alligator and listed it as a first-class endangered species, thereby providing it governmental protection.

Breeding stations have also been established, and local residents are now paid a bounty to capture alligators and bring them to one of these farms instead of killing them.

Elizabeth Sirimarco

See also Crocodiles and Gharials.

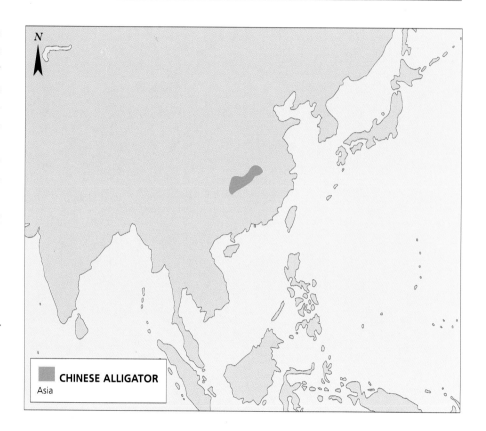

N

CHINESE ALLIGATOR
Asia

ALOES

Class: Angiosperm

Order: Liliopsida

Family: Aloaceae

Aloes are a large group of succulent plants with about 200 species. Although many of these are native to southern Africa, they are also found in Madagascar, East Africa, the Arabian peninsula, and the Canary Islands.

Their distinctive succulent leaves are arranged in spirals, but there is a wide diversity of shape and size among these plants. They range in size from tiny stemless rosette plants, such as *Aloe rauhii*, to trees, such as one that grows in Namibia, called *Aloe pillansii* that sometimes reaches up to 33 feet (10 meters) tall.

Aloe flowers are usually various shades of orange or red. These attractive plants can be seen in nurseries and botanical gardens and will be familiar to many people as household potted plants.

Aloe cosmetic, dietary, and medicinal products have also become household items.

Aloe vera is the main species that is grown commercially for the use and trade in its extracts. These plants are used in drinks and medicinal products. The species has been traded for centuries, and its wild origin is now obscure.

Another important species is *Aloe ferox*, which is the main source of the drug known as bitter aloe. *Aloe ferox* is a common South African plant and is still harvested from the wild.

Other species of aloe are now very rare and under threat in the wild as a result of habitat loss and habitat degradation, as well as over-collection. At present it is thought that 156 species, which account for over one third of the total number of aloe species, are considered by the IUCN to be threatened.

Aloe Albiflora

IUCN: Endangered

Leaves: Up to 6 in. (15 cm) long, covered in white spots, margins with soft teeth

Flowers: Raceme of white flowers on a stalk about 12 in. (30 cm) long

Habitat: Grasslands

Range: Madagascar

THE SMALL, SUCCULENT *Aloe albiflora* is very distinctive. One of the 600 endemic succulent plants of Madagascar, it is found only in Toliara and is considered to be endangered. Collecting for international trade has been one of the main threats to this species. During the 1980s many plants of aloe and euphorbia were collected and exported to Europe, Japan, and the United States

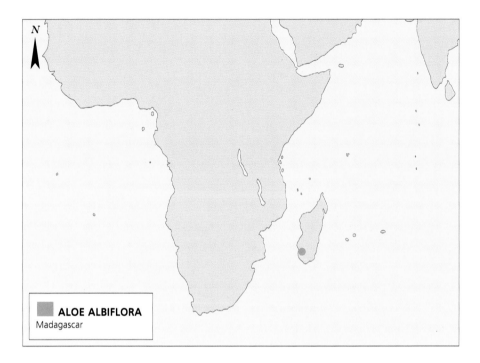

ALOE ALBIFLORA
Madagascar

natural habitat *Aloe bowiea* faces many threats, and its future is far from secure.

Temporary safety

Clearance of land for agriculture and overgrazing, especially in times of drought, have a negative effect on the places where *Aloe bowiea* grows.

Fortunately one population is on a privately owned game reserve and another is on land owned by a farmer who is sympathetic to conservation. There is always a fear, however, that this land will be sold for building purposes or development.

Another threat to *Aloe bowiea* is collecting by succulent enthusiasts. Although the plant is protected by law, unscrupulous collectors are not always deterred by this.

from Madagascar as nursery plants. This led to major concerns about the impact of the trade on Madagascar's unique flora. As a consequence, *Aloe albiflora* and a group of Madagascar's other miniature aloe species were given strict international protection in 1994. They are listed in Appendix I of the Convention on International Trade in Endangered Species of Wild Flora and Fauna (CITES).

The other major threat to *Aloe albiflora* is fire. Every year the grasslands of Madagascar are burned to improve the pasture for the prized zebu cattle. People in Madagascar measure their wealth by the number of zebu they own, and many rituals and ceremonies are based on the cattle. Unfortunately the burning destroys many of the special plants of the island.

Long-term protection of the habitat of *Aloe albiflora* is necessary to save the species. Growing more of the plants in nurseries will also help to take the pressure off wild populations.

Aloe Bowiea

IUCN: Endangered

Leaves: Pale green with soft white prickles, small white spots on the undersurfaces, margins have soft white prickles
Flower: Produced irregularly throughout the year, with a peak between October and March; greenish white flowers are arranged in a raceme
Habitat: Succulent-dominated grasslands
Range: South Africa

ALOE BOWIEA IS A very rare dwarf aloe known only from three sites in Eastern Cape Province of South Africa. It is a small, stemless succulent that grows in rocky soils along with other succulent plants such as *Euphorbia, Cotyledon, Crassula, Pachypodium,* and the pebble-like mesems. In its

ALOE BOWIEA
Africa

Aloe Dhufarensis

Height: Up to 5 ft. (1.5 m)
Leaves: Basal, arranged spirally, 16–20 in. (41–51 cm) long, flat above, convex beneath, with smooth margins
Flowers: In June. The inflorescences grow to about 3 ft. (1 m) with 1 to 2 branches; flowers red to yellow arranged in racemes
Habitat: Dry habitats
Range: Oman

ALOE DHUFARENSIS
Asia

ALOE DHUFARENSIS IS a perennial, stemless succulent herb. It is a striking plant with tall spikes of red to yellow flowers.

This rare aloe is found in drier areas of Dhofar in southern Oman. It is one of three aloe species growing in the area, the others being *Aloe whitcombei* and the much more widespread *Aloe inermis. Aloe dhufarensis* is plentiful in Wadi Adonib, the region in Oman where it was first discovered, but there is some concern that road building or other development projects could threaten its survival.

The species is collected by gardeners because it has attractive leaves and is able to survive in poor alkaline soils with little water. *Aloe dhufarensis* is also collected for local use as a medicinal plant. Juice from the leaves has been used to cure a range of ailments including headaches, aching limbs, diabetes, and constipation. The juice is also used as a cosmetic to decorate the face, neck, arms, and legs, dyeing them orange yellow.

The way in which the juice is collected is to snap off the leaves at the base of the plant, arrange them around a container or hollow scraped in the ground, and wait for the juice to drain out. The juice is then collected with a scoop or piece of bark and left to dry. Leather containers filled with dried aloe juice are sold in the markets of Dhofar.

This species of aloe is in cultivation at the Sultan Qaboos University Botanic Garden. No other conservation measures are thought to be in place at present.

Aloe Distans

Height: Up to 10 ft. (3 m) long
Stems: Creep along ground
Leaves: Up to 6 in. (15 cm) long, roughly triangular
Flowers: In December. Dull orange-red to bright red flowers arranged in short, tightly packed racemes
Habitat: Coastlines
Range: Cape Province, South Africa

The firm yellowish teeth of *Aloe distans* appear to be formidable deterrents to prospective collectors.

ALOE DISTANS IS a perennial with many sprawling stems that creep along the ground. The slightly fleshy, triangular leaves are bluish green with whitish spots and firm yellowish teeth.

This species has a fairly restricted distribution along the west coast of South Africa, stretching from Danger Point north to St. Helena Bay.

Aloe distans is not widely cultivated and does not grow well outside its natural habitats.

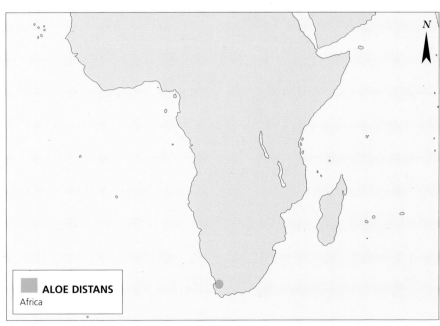

N

ALOE DISTANS
Africa

Aloe Jucunda

IUCN: Endangered

Height: Up to 14 in.
(36 cm) tall
Leaves: Dark green, 1½ in.
(4 cm) long and ¾–2 in.
(2–5 cm) wide with numerous
transparent spots and
marginal teeth
Flowers: Pale rose to coral
pink tubular flowers
Habitat: Forests
Range: Somalia

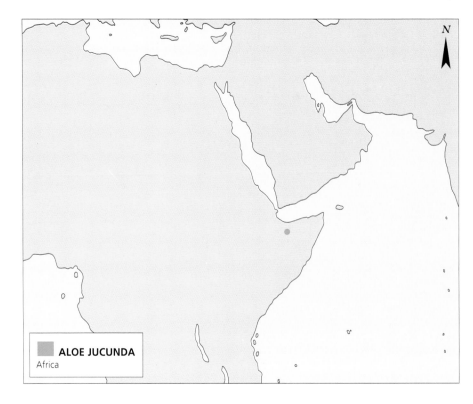

ALOE JUCUNDA

Africa

ALOE JUCUNDA IS a short-stemmed perennial, one of the 27 aloes that occur in Somalia. It is valued as an attractive succulent and is produced in nurseries for succulents.

It is not thought to be collected from the wild for trade. No

Aloe jucunda has distinctive pale pink tubular flowers. It is protected in a forest reserve in Somalia that may soon be declared a national park.

particular threats to the species are known at present.

Aloe jucunda grows in the Gaan Libah Forest Reserve, which is a priority area for succulent plant conservation in the IUCN/Species Survival Commission Conservation Action Plan for Cactus and Succulent

Plants. It has been proposed that the Gaan Libah Forest Reserve be declared a national park.

Aloe Ortholopha

IUCN: Endangered

Height: Up to 35 in.
(90 cm)
Leaves: Fleshy, growing from
central point with no stem
Flowers: Deep red, crimson,
or orange, growing along a
horizontal flower stalk
Pollination: By insect
Habitat: Grassy areas of
the Great Dyke
Range: Zimbabwe

ALOE ORTHOLOPHA IS a strikingly attractive species of aloe. The plant, which has rosette-patterned leaves , is stemless, but the inflorescence grows up to 35 inches (90 centimeters) tall. The

The leaves of *Aloe ortholopha* are arranged in a rosette formation, with the inflorescence springing from it.

flowers range from deep red or crimson to orange and grow along a horizontal flower stalk. The flowering period is July to August. Pollination for *Aloe ortholopha* is thought to be carried out by insects.

Aloe ortholopha is found only in Zimbabwe, where its distribution is restricted to a small area of the Great Dyke. This is an ancient ridge of serpentine rock that runs for over 300 miles (500 kilometers), rising steeply above the surrounding countryside. The Great Dyke has been identified as a Center of Plant Diversity by the World Conservation Union. *Aloe ortholopha* has adapted to the serpentine soils, which are rich in minerals such as magnesium. It grows in grassy areas with other species of aloe and succulent euphorbias.

The Great Dyke holds the world's largest deposits of chrome, and mining for this ore has been one of the main threats to *Aloe ortholopha*. All species of aloe are protected by Zimbabwe's conservation legislation. It is illegal to collect plants from the wild. *Aloe ortholopha* grows from seed and is now in cultivation in various parts of the world.

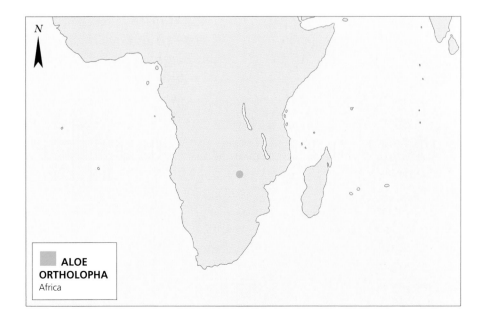

ALOE ORTHOLOPHA
Africa

Aloe Pillansii

IUCN: Endangered

Height: Up to 33 ft. (10 m) tall
Leaves: 20–24 in. (51–61 cm) long and 4–4¾ in. (10–12 cm) wide, with white teeth
Flowers: Bright yellow tubular flowers, borne in branched heads
Habitat: Arid, sparsely vegetated land
Range: Namibia, South Africa (Northern Cape)

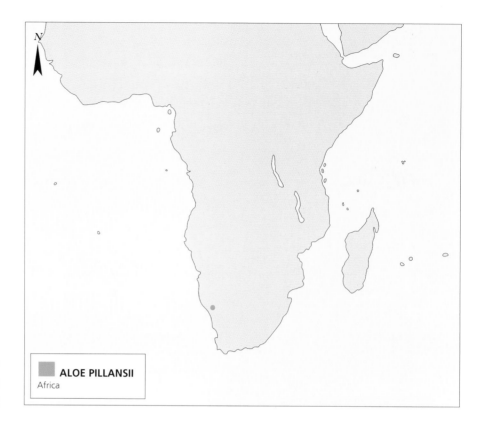

ALOE PILLANSII
Africa

THE TREE ALOE plays a very important role in the harsh ecosystem where it occurs. *Aloe pillansii* grows in the extremely hot and dry Richtersveld area of Northern Cape, South Africa. The distribution of the species also extends into similar areas of neighboring Namibia.

Only a few perennial plants can survive the tough climate, so *Aloe pillansii* provides an important source of shelter, nectar, food, and water, particularly for birds.

Unfortunately *Aloe pillansii* is endangered, and fewer than 200 individual plants of this species are now known to survive in the wild. The older plants are dying and new plants are not found. There is evidence that baboons and porcupines gnaw the stems of the remaining plants. Goats and donkeys may also be damaging the plants. Collection from the wild for succulent plant

Aloe striata, which is classified by the IUCN as rare, can be found in Karoo Gardens, in Worcester, South Africa.

The rare kraal aloe (*Aloe asperifolia*) has adapted to the extremely arid conditions of its environment in Namib-Naukluft Park in Namibia, Africa.

growers is another threat to this species. *Aloe pillansii* is protected by law in South Africa and is included in Appendix 1 of the Convention on International Trade in Endangered Species of Wild Fauna and Flora (CITES). Fortunately this species of aloe is easily grown from seed, and large numbers of plants are in cultivation around the world. There has, however, been recent evidence of trade in wild-collected plants, especially to Japan.

The habitat of the species falls within the recently declared Richtersveld National Park. Additional measures may, however, be necessary to ensure the recovery of the species in the wild, and a survey is needed to find out if there are more remaining plants in Namibia.

ALOE POLYPHYLLA IS a succulent perennial with a stem growing to 4 inches (10 centimeters). It is highly valued by succulent plant enthusiasts because of the symmetrically arranged rosettes of leaves. Collecting from the wild has been a major threat to the

Aloe Polyphylla

IUCN: Endangered

Height: 19½–23½ in. (50–60 cm)
Stem: 4 in. (10 cm)
Leaves: Mature plants have 75–100 leaves in tight rosettes 20–24 in. (51–61 cm) across
Flowers: August to December. 1–1½ in. (3–4 cm) long, green with purple tips, on stalks 20–24 in. (51–61 cm)
Flowering season: August to December
Habitat: Rich peat soils in mountain habitats
Range: Lesotho

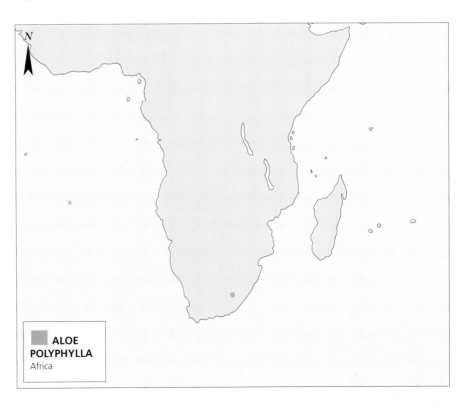

ALOE POLYPHYLLA
Africa

species. Unfortunately plants collected from the wild do not survive well, so the pressure on wild populations has remained. Despite it being listed on Appendix I of CITES, there is recent evidence of an illegal international trade in *Aloe polyphylla*. The plants are also used for medicinal purposes by the local Basotho people.

The spiral aloe is endemic to Lesotho in southern Africa. It grows in scattered localities throughout this small country but with concentrations in the Thaba Putsoa Range and the Maseru area of the Drakensberg Mountains.

The species grows at altitudes of up to 7,300–8,920 feet (2,230–2,720 meters) on steep basalt slopes with loose rock. It is able to withstand freezing temperatures and does not grow well in warm or hot, dry climates.

The malachite sunbird is one of the pollinators of *Aloe polyphylla*. A large amount of seed is produced but only a small proportion of it germinates. Very few seedlings are seen in the wild.

The spiral aloe is Lesotho's national flower. It has been protected by law in the country since 1938. It has been recommended that a national park be established for the species, where it could be protected from grazing animals.

Increased cultivation will help to take the pressure off wild populations, but unfortunately some enthusiasts of succulent plants continue to break the law and demand wild-collected aloes.

This fine tree aloe (*Aloe pillansii*) is one example of the diverse forms of this species. It provides shelter, nectar, food, and water for other wildlife.

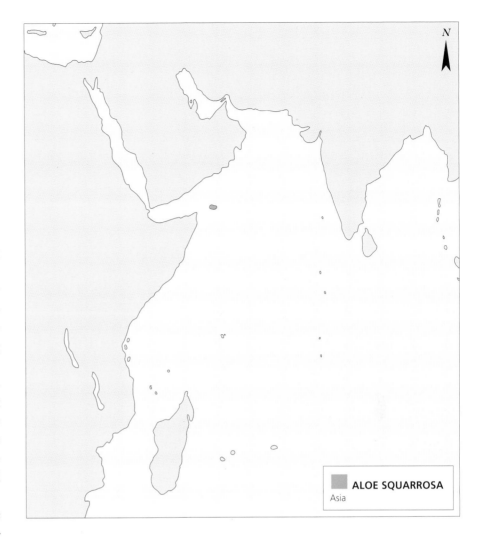

ALOE SQUARROSA
Asia

Aloe Squarrosa

IUCN: Endangered

Stems: Thin, up to 16 in. (41 cm) long
Leaves: Light green, 3 in. (8 cm) long, ¾ in. (2 cm) wide, with white spots and sharp teeth
Flowers: Red tubular on short stalks
Habitat: Limestone cliffs
Range: Socotra, off the Horn of Africa

ALOE SQUARROSA IS a perennial succulent plant that can be found hanging from rock faces. It branches from the base, and the leaves are green with white spots and toothed edges. The leaves are arranged in loose rosettes. The plant has red tubular flowers. This is an attractive species that could become a popular plant if more widely grown by plant nurseries. *Aloe squarrosa* is grown by some botanical gardens such as the Royal Botanic Gardens, Kew, in England.

Aloe squarrosa is confined to Yemen's island of Socotra, off the Horn of Africa. It grows there only on limestone cliffs in a very small area in the northwest of the island. This limestone area is commonly covered in cloud. When *Aloe squarrosa* was first discovered in 1880, only two plants were found. More plants have been found in the wild over the

Aloe rauhii has been classified by the IUCN–The World Conservation Union as rare. This species lives in Madagascar, along with other endangered species.

years but the species survives in critically low numbers.

The main threat to this species, and to the other unique plants of Socotra, is from grazing by goats. The people who live on the island are mainly subsistence farmers who grow food such as dates, millet, and sweet potatoes for their own use, and they keep goats. The island has no roads, no industry, and no medical facilities. Socotra has about 260 plant species that are endemic to the island, and many of these are threatened with extinction.

Ten of the plant species that grew only in the small area where *Aloe squarrosa* occurs are now thought to be extinct. No land is specifically protected for nature conservation on Socotra.

Some traditional practices on the island, such as livestock management to prevent overgrazing, are favorable to the conservation of rare plants. Many of the islanders recognize the importance of vegetation to support their way of life.

There is no specific protection for *Aloe squarrosa*. It has been recommended that the limestone cliffs where it occurs be made into a nature reserve.

Protecting the island's unique flora will become more urgent if Socotra is developed with roads and port facilities. Socotra has been identified as a Center of Plant Diversity by the IUCN–The World Conservation Union.

This colorful specimen, *Aloe krapohliana* (left), is a vulnerable species that is found in Namaqualand in southwestern Africa.

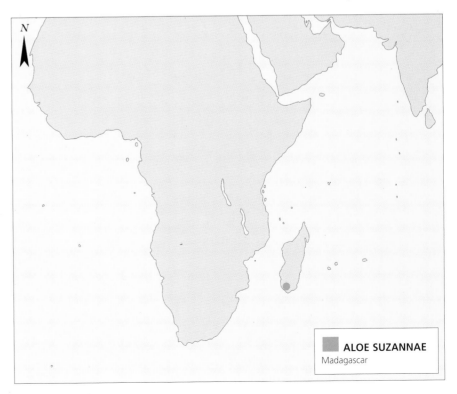

ALOE SUZANNAE
Madagascar

Aloe Suzannae

IUCN: Endangered

Height: Solitary stems
10–26 ft. (3–8 m) tall
Leaves: 31–39 in. (80–100 cm)
long, with rounded tips and
yellowish teeth, arranged in a
rosette at the top of the stem
Flowers: Yellow and numerous,
carried on erect stems up to
11½ ft. (3.5 m) long
Habitat: Sandy habitats
Range: Madagascar

ALOE SUZANNAE is confined to small areas of sandy shore habitats in the Amboasary region and Itampolo in southwestern Mada-gascar. A few plants grow on large rocks near Behara. Only a few adult plants are known in each population, and there is no sign of young plants growing in the area.

The species is very rarely traded, but seed or young plants have been occasionally sold to collectors of succulents.

The plant is too big for the collections of most succulent plant enthusiasts, so there is less risk of their being collected from the wild than for the smaller Madagascan aloes.

The species was, however, included in Appendix I of CITES in 1994 because any international trade in wild plants would be very damaging to the survival of the species.

Habitat destruction is the main threat faced by *Aloe suzannae*. Forest fires are a major problem. The establishment of a nature reserve would help to ensure the survival of this species. It has also been suggested that seed-grown plants be carefully reintroduced into the wild to reinforce existing populations. At present many of the remaining plants are too widely scattered to ensure effective pollination.

Aloe Whitcombei

IUCN: Endangered

Height: Up to 8 in. (20 cm)
Leaves: Pale green with spots
Flowers: White flowers
arranged in a raceme on a stalk
about 4 in. (10 cm) long
Habitat: Clefts in sea cliffs
Range: Oman

ALOE WHITCOMBEI is a perennial succulent herb that is endemic to Dhofar, where it is found at only one location. It grows in clefts in sea cliffs, which are affected by mist. It is thought that the entire population consists of fewer than 100 plants.

Collection of wild plants or habitat disturbance could decimate the species.

This species of aloe is in cultivation at the Sultan Qaboos University Botanic Garden.

Sara Oldfield

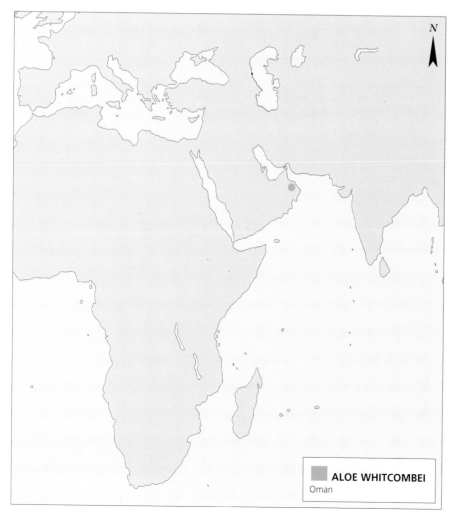

ALOE WHITCOMBEI
Oman

A close up (right) of *Aloe distans* shows the long, triangular-shaped leaves, densely covered with teeth-like spines.

Anguila Ciega
(Ophisternon infernale)

IUCN: Endangered

Class: Actinopterygii
Order: Synbranchiformes
Family: Synbranchidae
Length: 10 in. (25 cm)
Reproduction: Egg layer
Habitat: Underground waterways
Range: Yucatán Peninsula, Mexico

ANGUILA CIEGA
Mexico

THE UNUSUAL anguila ciega is a fish found on the Yucatán Peninsula in the Mexican states of Yucatán and Quintana Roo. Because of its exceedingly small range and the threats to its last remaining habitat, the anguila ciega is considered by the IUCN to be endangered.

The Spanish word *anguila* means "eel," which is very appropriate. The sleek body of this fish is shaped like a snake, with a head that is only slightly larger in diameter than its tail. The anguila ciega is blind and has no skin pig-

The anguila ciega bears a strong resemblance to an eel, which is also a species of fish.

mentation; this is the result of spending much of its time in underground waterways away from sunlight.

Cave habitat
Water-filled caves offer conditions that are very different from those at the surface. Cave-dwelling animals live in total darkness in an energy-poor environment. Caves cannot sustain green plants, which capture sunlight and turn it into food for other plants and animals. Because of their isolation from the surface and the lack of life-giving sunlight, subterranean fish depend completely on food that comes from the surface to their underground domain. Food may be carried in water that enters the cave from the surface. Some cave dwellers live off guano produced by bats that roost in caves.

In addition to the absence of light, caves have a stable temperature that usually corresponds with the average yearly temperature at the surface. Because of this difference, fish like the anguila ciega can develop a metabolism that is less tolerant of environmental changes, a feature that may limit its ability to expand its range.

Because the anguila ciega is blind, it relies heavily on a complex array of other sensory organs; touch, taste, and smell are extremely important.

As a subterranean species with a small range, the anguila ciega would be severely affected by any changes in the quality of the water in which it lives or in its food supply. Protecting this fish's habitat is especially important to its survival.

William E. Manci

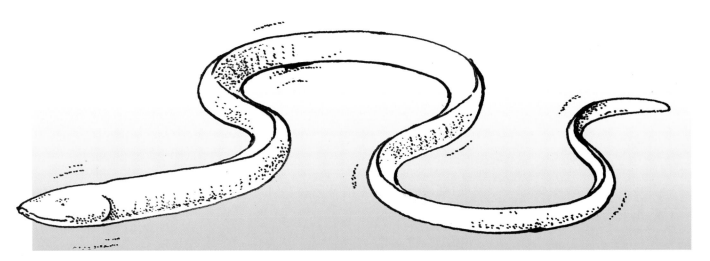

ANOAS

Class: Mammalia

Order: Artiodactyla

Family: Bovidae

Subfamily: Bovini

Southeast Asia is the home of a number of dwarf cattle. These animals are found in tropical rain forests on mainland Asia and on many Indonesian islands. The lowland anoa and the mountain anoa are both primarily nocturnal animals, each preferring the terrain that gives it its name. Anoas are related to other endangered cattle, including the Asiatic water buffalo and the tamaraw.

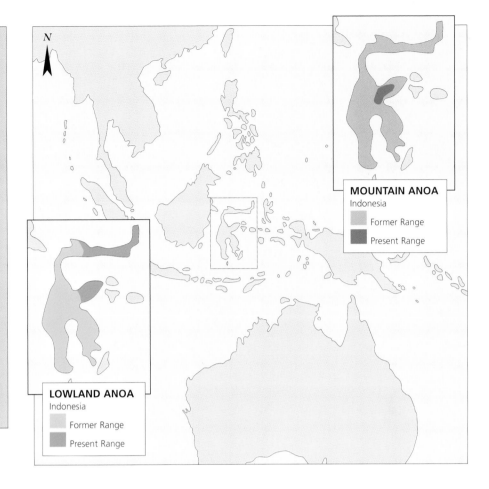

MOUNTAIN ANOA
Indonesia

Former Range

Present Range

LOWLAND ANOA
Indonesia

Former Range

Present Range

Lowland Anoa

(Bubalus depressicornis)

ESA: Endangered

IUCN: Endangered

Weight: 640–685 lb.
(290–310 kg)

Shoulder height: 31½–35½ in.
(80–90 cm)

Diet: Grasses, leaves, shoots

Gestation period: 275–315 days

Longevity: 20–25 years

Habitat: Deep rain forest

Range: Island of Sulawesi
(Celebes), Indonesia

THE LOWLAND ANOA is a dwarf cattle whose outer appearance illustrates its successful adaptation to a tropical rain forest habitat. The color of this bovine's hide can vary from a very light tan to almost black. Its skin and coat tend to be oily, helping it shed outer moisture in a damp and wet tropical climate. Its short legs and relatively small hooves give it good footing through the rain forest.

Lowland anoa tend to be very shy and are primarily solitary. Occasionally pairs are seen, but most often this is either a breeding pair or a cow with her most recent calf.

Tough when cornered

Anoa are very quick to retreat into the bush when disturbed. They rely on their ability to disappear into the heavy vegetation for their protection; however, when they are cornered, they will stay and fight, and do surprisingly well. Wild dogs occasionally prey on them, but the primary threat to their survival is humans. The biggest problem for the low-land anoa is the destruction of its habitat, when rain forest is cut down and destroyed. The lowland anoa really has no vast range in which to retreat because it is found only on the Indonesian island of Sulawesi (Celebes), and therefore it is very vulnerable to the destruction of the forest. The lowland anoa has declined to the point that it is listed as an endangered species.

The anoa in captivity

Lowland anoa have been kept in captivity in both Europe and North America with reasonable success. However, the number brought into captivity has been limited, resulting in a relatively narrow gene pool. This means that the population just barely maintains itself. The gene pool needs to be enlarged in order to ensure a healthy future for a cap-

tive population that can be drawn upon in the future to reintroduce these animals to safe areas.

Mountain Anoa
(Bubalus quarlesi)

ESA: Endangered
IUCN: Endangered

Weight: 415–465 lb.
(190–210 kg)
Shoulder height: 27½–31½ in.
(70–80 cm)
Diet: Grasses, leaves, shoots
Gestation period: 270–310 days
Longevity: 20 years
Habitat: Montane forest
Range: Island of Sulawesi (Celebes), Indonesia

THE MOUNTAIN ANOA, like the lowland anoa, lives only on the island of Sulawesi in Indonesia. The characteristics of both are fairly similar: both are wild cattle, or bovines, and both are short, stocky, and streamlined. Their skin is relatively oily, which helps them shed outer moisture in damp rain forest environments. The mountain anoa seems to be a uniform dark brown to black, with some variation in color. Both types of anoa tend to be solitary and are most active at night. When their habitat was less disturbed than it is now, anoas displayed diurnal (active during daytime) habits.

The anoa is a shy and elusive animal that hides when disturbed. Hunting and degradation of this species' habitat have reduced population numbers to the point where the animal is now endangered.

Anoas are found in the rapidly disappearing rain forests of Sulawesi (Celebes) in Indonesia.

The short, stocky legs and even-toed hooves of the mountain anoa give it a surefooted ability to climb the rugged hills and low mountains of Sulawesi. The anoa is endangered primarily because of hunting and the loss of its habitat. Since it is restricted to just one island population, there is nowhere else for it to go. Its situation in the wild is very precarious.

In captivity, mountain anoas have been kept in fewer numbers than lowland anoas with about the same level of success. Although the mountain anoa will breed in captivity and do reasonably well, there are so few individuals that the gene pool is dangerously small.

Warren D. Thomas

See also Asian Water Buffalo, Tamaraw.

Culebra Island Giant Anole

(Anolis roosevelti)

ESA: Endangered

IUCN: Critically endangered

Class: Reptilia
Order: Sauria
Family: Iguanidae
Length: 6 in. (15.2 cm)
Clutch size: Unknown
Incubation: Unknown
Diet: Probably figs
Habitat: Presumably arboreal
Range: Endemic to Culebra Island in the Caribbean Sea

THE CULEBRA ISLAND giant anole is a lizard that was first described in 1931 on the basis of one specimen collected by a local child. Although it was the only available specimen, biologists were quite certain that it represented a new species. While it possessed similar characteristics to two other anoles found on the Puerto Rican mainland and the Island of Hispaniola, it was distinct from both. In 1932, a second specimen was collected

CULEBRA ISLAND GIANT ANOLE
Culebra Island, Puerto Rico

that provided additional information to differentiate it from other species of anole. Unfortunately, this was the last specimen to be seen by biologists.

Elusive lizard

The natural history and ecology of the Culebra Island giant anole are unknown, and the species has been virtually ignored since its discovery. Because a specimen has not been collected since 1932, many biologists believe that the giant anole may be extinct. There is some reason, however, to believe it still exists on the island.

To determine whether the Culebra Island giant anole is extinct, several herpetologists have searched the island without success. It is thought, however, that the remaining patches of virgin forest could support small numbers of lizards. Because the species apparently lives in trees, it is protected from a number of would-be predators. Before listing the species as extinct, further surveys must be conducted and the remaining habitats protected. The U.S. Fish and Wildlife Service currently lists the lizard as endangered, and the remaining forest on Culebra Island is considered to be critical habitat.

This anole is a brownish gray lizard with two lines on each side, one beginning near the ear and extending to the groin, the other beginning at the shoulder and extending to the groin. Its eyelids are yellow, and the throat fan is gray except for the lower rear quarter, which is light yellow. The underside of the belly is whitish. The tail is scalloped, supporting a large fin along most of its length. The scientific name hon-

ors Theodore Roosevelt, Jr., who was governor of Puerto Rico at the time the Culebra Island giant anole was discovered.

Possible recovery plans

Scientists can only guess the reason for the scarcity of this anole. Presumably, extensive deforestation of the island is the major problem. There are a number of animals that could be potential predators of the lizard, including larger lizards, birds, and snakes. Along with attempts to determine whether the anole is extinct, there are plans to begin a recovery program to help reestablish it on Culebra Island. The most important issues are maintaining what is left of the lizard's forest habitat and learning more about its ecology.

To accomplish the goals of a recovery plan approved by the U.S. Fish and Wildlife Service, efforts to confirm the existence of the species must be increased. The plan provides for three or more field surveys per year.

Habitat protection

If the existence of the Culebra Island giant anole can be confirmed, a full-fledged recovery plan can begin. Continued field studies must identify the factors necessary for this species survival. Healthy population levels must be established and monitored to ensure that the number of lizards is either stable or increasing. Most important, agreements between government and private agencies must be formalized to guarantee continued protection of the remaining patches of forest habitat.

Elizabeth Sirimarco

See also Lizards.

Slender Antbird

(Rhopornis ardesiaca)

IUCN: Endangered

Class: Aves
Order: Passeriformes
Family: Thamnophilidae
Length: 6–6½ in. (15–16.5 cm)
Weight: Unknown
Clutch size: Unknown
Incubation: Unknown
Diet: Unknown
Habitat: Giant bromeliads in dry woodland edges
Range: Coastal ridge of Bahia, Brazil

The habitat of the slender antbird consists of giant bromeliad patches in dry woodland forests.

THE SLENDER ANTBIRD occupies the same woodland habitat used by the narrow-billed antwren (*Formicivora iheringi*) and is vulnerable to habitat alterations. By the end of the 1970s, the slender antbird was still easily found in localized populations. However, the rapid rate of converting woodland to grassland for grazing cattle suggests that the species may soon experience severe losses. This slender bird likes living in bromeliad patches. Two common species of bromeliads are the pineapple (*Ananas comosus*) and Spanish moss (*Tillandsia usneoides*). Many plants in the family Bromeliaceae are able to utilize sunlight to transform nutrients into food even in dark forests, since they can grow on the trees themselves, rather than needing to have their roots in soil. The number of slender antbirds in a given area depends on the size of bromeliad patches. Small bromeliad patches can harbor only a single pair; larger patches may sustain more.

Distinctive behavior

Unlike many species of their family, these antbirds do not follow ants. They hop about plants and on the ground as they search for insect prey. They tend to be quiet most of the time, although they utter low, one-syllable call notes as they move, probably to stay in touch with each other. The male slender antbirds have dark gray upperparts with black tails, throats, and upper breasts; females have a dark buffy crown and nape with a white throat.

By some accounts, the coastal forests of eastern Brazil have been almost totally destroyed. Perhaps only 1 to 3 percent of the original forest area survives today. Many species have already disappeared from this area of Brazil, including vertebrate and invertebrate animals and many different kinds of plants.

Despite legal protection, no specific remedial action has been taken to either stabilize or to attempt to recover this species from the threat of extinction.

Superkilling

Many philosophers who deal with environmental ethics consider extinction as so-called superkilling, because it involves the loss of every individual of a species. The changes in coastal Brazil represent more than simple extinction. They represent a kind of superkilling in which an entire ecosystem is being destroyed. With this kind of destruction, many species such as the slender antbird are lost before anything is ever learned about their natural importance.

Kevin Cook

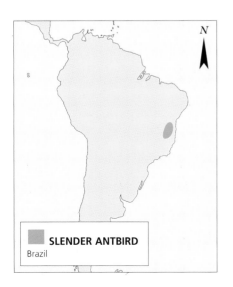

SLENDER ANTBIRD
Brazil

Giant Anteater

(Myrmecophaga tridactyla)

IUCN: Vulnerable

Class: Mammalia
Order: Xenarthra
Family: Myrmecophagidae
Weight: 40–86 lb. (18–39 kg)
Head-body length: 39–47 in. (100–120 cm)
Diet: All life stages of ants and termites; beetle larvae
Gestation period: 190 days
Longevity: 25 years in captivity
Habitat: Savanna, grassland, wet forests, and swamps
Range: Central America to northern Argentina

IN SOME AREAS of the world, ants and termites comprise fully 75 percent of the existing biomass. Moreover, at any given moment the number of ants and termites alive on this planet is greater than the number of human beings who have ever lived. No less than six different orders of mammals contain species that specialize in keeping these insects in check.

In addition to four species of anteaters, this group of specialized insectivores includes armadillos, pangolins, echidnas, aardwolves, numbats, and aardvarks. While most of these species eat both ants and termites, some exhibit a preference for one or the other. Many of these animals supplement their diets with lizards, other small animals, and vegetation, but such is not the case with *Myrmecophaga tridactyla*, the giant anteater of Central and South America. The biggest of four anteater species,

all exclusive to the Western hemisphere, the giant anteater is both a strange-looking creature and a model of efficiency. At up to 86 pounds (39 kilograms) and measuring up to 7 feet long (2.1 meters) including the tail, it has been described only half in jest as looking like "a scaled-down Concorde jet on a skateboard with a big, plumed tail." Its pigeon-toed gait, which is assumed in order to protect its digging claws from becoming blunt, adds to the overall strangeness of its appearance. The hairs on its tail are long, giving the appendage a bushy or fanlike appearance. A distinctive black stripe extends from its throat across its shoulder to the midline and is bordered above and below by a white stripe. Its body is generally gray to brown to tawny. These features

make it easily distinguishable from its three smaller brethren: the two-toed or silky anteater, and both the northern and southern tamanduas.

Habitat

The giant anteater ranges from southern Guatemala to northern Argentina. It prefers areas of well-drained soil that support high ant and termite populations. It is active during the day in areas of low human inhabitation, but switches over to a more nocturnal lifestyle in areas where there is dense human populations. Like its smaller relatives, the giant anteater is able to climb. However, it usually chooses not to and seems to prefer to forage on the ground.

Teeth are entirely lacking in all four anteaters. Instead,

GIANT ANTEATER
Central America and
South America

anteaters have a long, tubelike snout with a slight down-turning arc and a long, worm-shaped tongue. Ants and termites do not require a lot of chewing, and the anteater uses its 2-foot (0.6-meter) tongue, which flicks in and out of its mouth twice a second, to catch many insects at a time. When feeding, the tongue is coated with a sticky saliva to which the prey adhere.

Efficient diggers

Like many other animals that prey on ants and termites, giant anteaters are highly efficient diggers. Unlike armadillos, the anteater does not merely unearth an ant or termite colony in order to commence feeding. Instead, it uses its front claws like scalpels to expose one room or tunnel at a time. Like cattle, it tends to graze for a few moments and then move on. Some researchers theorize that the anteater is a model citizen from an ecological standpoint. They claim it eats with minimal destruction to the environment—engaging in what is popularly known as prudent predation, which, simply put, means that it leaves some for later.

The giant anteater performs an important service—it keeps vast populations of ants and other insects under control.

Anteater repellent

Others dispute this view by citing the responses of the anteater's prey. Nonreproductive ants and termites consist of two castes—workers and soldiers. Workers are thought to be the anteater's favored food source, although soldiers are also eaten. Under attack, soldiers either secrete or sometimes spray the anteater with a noxious repellent. In a matter of a few moments after the colony is attacked, large numbers of soldiers gather in defense and the levels of secretion increase, discouraging the anteater. At that point, the anteater is thought to cease feeding and move on to another mound nearby.

The powerful forelegs are equipped with long, sharp claws that can function as weapons as well as feeding tools. In self-defense, the giant anteater sits on its powerful hind legs and, balanced in part by its bushy tail, either strikes out with its sharp claws or hugs and claws the predator's back. Reports exist of dogs and jaguars completely disemboweled by anteaters. Citizens and scientists have told tales of dead jaguars and anteaters locked in a death grip.

Lifestyle

Although reports exist of gestation periods as short as 142 days, typically the single young is born after a gestation period of 190 days. Early in its development, the offspring is carried from shelter to shelter on its mother's back; however, as the young begins to mature, it is carried to feeding sites out in the open. During this period the young anteater is thought to be especially vulnerable to predators.

Giant anteaters are solitary animals that were not thought to be very territorial. However, recent studies have reported that many hostile interactions occur between males. Females seem to tolerate a higher degree of range overlap, but disagreements over the size of the home range (estimates range from 1¼ to 15 square miles, or 3.25 to 39 square kilometers), make any conclusions tentative.

These animals live in a region of the world in which the forests and hills are being drastically altered for agricultural use. As brush and shrubbery are increasingly cut back, the anteater is deprived of shelter and becomes more vulnerable to predation. Giant anteaters are doubly affected by habitat loss, because while their food supply decreases, their risk of attack by predators increases.

Renardo Barden
and Terry Tompkins

ANTELOPES

Class: Mammalia

Order: Artiodactyla

Family: Bovidae

Subfamily: Hippotraginae

Antelope, bison, buffalo, cattle, goats, and sheep are all part of the Bovidae family that is found on every continent in the Northern Hemisphere. There are some 138 species in wild and domesticated forms. Their most distinctive feature is their hooves, which have only two well-developed digits.

Bovids can be found in many different types of terrain: grassland, tundra, desert, forests, and even swamps. Antelopes seem to prefer grasslands and open forests.

All bovids are grass eaters, grazing for food and then digesting it by chewing it twice: once when they bite off the grass or leaves, and again when they chew the cud brought up from their stomach system before they swallow it again for the last time.

Four-horned Antelope

(Tetracerus quadricornis)

IUCN: Endangered

Weight: 37½–48½ lb. (17–22 kg)

Shoulder height: About 25 in. (64 cm)

Diet: Leaves, bulbs, shoots, grasses

Gestation period: 240–255 days

Longevity: About 10 years

Habitat: Grasslands to open forest

Range: India and Nepal

THE FOUR-HORNED antelope is an unusual little Indian ungulate (hoofed animal). It is dull brown with a darker stripe down the front legs. Its underparts are light. The local name for this unusual animal is *chowsingha*. By nature it is very wary, and because of persecution by humans it has become even more so. It is found in open woodlands and grasslands, always near water. Unlike many other antelope, its need for open, available water is critical.

Four-horned antelope have a number of glands that are used to mark territory and to meet other social needs. There is a promi-nent gland located between the rear hooves, two others in the inguinal area, and one on the face below each eye. Glands for mark-ing territory are a common feature of many antelope species.

Horns

The most remarkable thing about this antelope is that it is the only truly four-horned mammal. There are other animals such as several different varieties of domestic sheep that are referred to as four-horned; however, they are in reality two-horned sheep that have the unusual character-istic of having horns that split when they start to grow. Each half grows in a different direc-tion, giving the sheep the appearance of having four horns.

Another animal that is often referred to as multi-horned is the giraffe. They are even called two-horned, three-horned, or five-horned, depending on the species. The horns on the giraffe are bony protrubances of the skull, and they are covered with skin. This means they do not con-stitute true horns. A true horn consists of a bony projection from the skull called a cornual process that is covered by a con-tinually growing hard substance that we call horn. The horns on the *chowsingha* are only present on the male. They consist of two horns high on the head near the ears and two forward on the head above the eyes. The rear horns are always the longest, usually an average of about 2 inches (5 cen-timeters) each. The largest horns on record are 7½ inches (19 cen-timeters). The front set of horns are not always obvious. Only about 30 to 40 percent of the males show well-defined sets of horns. The rest possess the obvi-ous rear set; the front set are buried in the fur and are invisi-ble. The horns are dark and are not ringed like many other ante-lope, but they do have an anterior keel, or forward ridge.

Breeding

The young can be born almost any month of the year with the highest concentration arriving during October to February. Breeding takes place during the hot season and the rainy season. The gestation period is eight to eight and a half months, or 240 to 255 days. The female has from one to three calves. The calves are dependent on the mother for six to eight months, although sometimes they will

Unlike 30 to 40 percent of male antelopes, the female four-horned antelope does not possess any horns.

stay with her until she drives them away at her next estrus (the next fertile period).

Habits and habitat

The four-horned antelope's favorite habitat is open, hilly forests always close to water. They are diurnally active and are commonly solitary, although it is not unusual to see pairs. This shows a loose social bonding. They are capable of very quick movement and their gait is characteristically jerky.

Captive population

Four-horned antelope have rarely been kept in captivity. They are not easy to capture and they are stress-prone, so they must be handled carefully. When they have been properly managed, they do very well in captivity; examples are the group at the zoo in Paris and the one at the Jardin des Plantes. There is another breeding group at the estate of John Aspinall at Howletts in England, with the largest group in England at Bekesborne in Kent. Another small group is kept at the Berlin zoo. Captive animals become quite habituated and tame, but they still retain their flight reflex.

Protection needed

Although they have a very large range over much of India, in the wild they are endangered and in some areas are nearly extinct due to destruction of both animals and habitat. Their meat is sought by the local populations. The Indian government offers them some protection, but it has been ineffective. Laws must be enforced to ensure their survival.

Warren D. Thomas

Giant Sable Antelope

(Hippotragus niger variani)

ESA: Endangered

IUCN: Critically endangered

Weight: 550–620 lb. (250–280 kg)
Shoulder height: 50–60 in. (130–150 cm)
Diet: Grasses, leaves, twigs
Gestation period: 270–290 days
Longevity: 18–20 years
Habitat: Open forest, grasslands
Range: Angola

THERE ARE FEW animals in nature that are as spectacular and elegantly beautiful as the giant sable antelope. It is part of a group of species known as horselike antelopes, and, when seen from a distance, the giant sable antelope is often thought to resemble a horse or pony. Its powerful shoulders and heavy neck muscles support a black-and-white face crowned by a sweeping, arched set of horns. Its overall appearance is quite imposing.

The giant sable is one of three types of sable antelopes found in Africa. The smallest is the Roosevelt sable (*Hippotragus niger roosevelti*) found in Kenya. The common sable (*H. niger niger*) is found in southern Africa. The giant sable lives in the grassland and open forests of the Angolan highlands.

The giant sable differs from the common sable in facial markings; otherwise they are generally the same color. Young females are

a chestnut to a reddish color, which in time tends to darken until they become almost as dark as the bulls.

The bulls are very dark, almost purplish black, which contrasts vividly with the white markings on their rump, belly, and face. Both males and females are equipped with a formidable set of horns.

Giant horns

The giant sable is not known as a giant antelope because of its size; its bulk does not vary very much from that of the common sable. It is referred to as giant because of the great sweep of horns that reaches over its back. The world's record measures an incredible 64 inches (162.5 centimeters) long.

The giant sable antelope has never been numerous, because it lives in a very restricted area of Angola. Its habits in the wild seem much like the other two forms of sable antelope.

It has the ability to run very fast but does not rely on its speed merely for its own preservation. It is an inquisitive animal and, when surprised, will run a short

The facial markings, the shape of its head, and its impressive horns make this sable antelope stand out anywhere.

distance then stop and turn to see what made it start running.

Both males and females defend themselves extremely well with their great horns, and because of this most predators tend to leave them alone. Occasionally a lion will take on the giant sable, but only if it is pressed by hunger. Lions will sometimes go after a young female, calf, or very old animal. They tend to leave mature bulls and cows alone, simply because they defend themselves so effectively. Packs of hunting dogs are known to attack lone sables, but there have been a number of accounts of a lone bull sable defending itself successfully against such a group of animals.

The giant sable antelope has learned to back its rump into a thorn thicket to protect itself from attack from the rear, then stand off hunting dogs with its formidable horns. A sable can strike downward, straight ahead, and butt its horns using its powerful neck muscles. It can also rake its horns sideways, using them like hooks. A predator might think it has wounded or killed a giant sable, only to end up dying on its horns.

Elusive animals

The common sable has been kept successfully in captivity; however, the giant sable has really never had a chance to breed in this way. The only time the giant sable has been kept in captivity was just after World War II, when two females were taken to a zoo in Lisbon, Portugal. A male was

never captured, and the two females simply lived out their lives there without breeding.

The giant sable antelope is classified by the (U.S.F.W.S.) as endangered in the wild and probably numbers no more than 1,000 individuals today. This species is restricted to only a small section of Angola, a country that has been in a state of turmoil for years, with both civil war and guerrilla warfare.

The future of the giant sable in the wild is precarious, and no captive population exists. For these reasons, this magnificent animal is critically endangered.

The Roosevelt sable antelope, *Hippotragus niger roosevelti*, is the smallest of the African sable species and makes its home in Kenya.

Hunter's Antelope

(Damaliscus hunteri)

IUCN: Critically endangered

Weight: 150–180 lb. (70–80 kg)
Shoulder height: 40–60 in. (100–150 cm)
Diet: Grasses
Gestation period: 270–290 days
Longevity: 12–15 years
Habitat: Grasslands
Range: Southwestern Somalia, eastern Kenya

HUNTER'S ANTELOPE is part of what is called the hartebeest tribe of animals. These are relatively tall antelopes with long faces and distinctive horns. The horns of Hunter's antelope are long, delicate and lyre-shaped, resembling the horns of an impala.

Speed and stamina

This is a true hartebeest, and like other hartebeests, Hunter's antelope has the ability to escape from danger by accelerating to surprising speeds. In addition to speed, it has a great deal of stamina and can outrun most other animals. It is a rare horse that can keep up with any of the hartebeest family for any length of time.

Because of its limited range, threats to Hunter's antelope's habitat makes this a critically endangered population. Over the years a number of plans have been proposed to construct dams in the area, which would obliterate much of the antelope's environment and place it in great jeopardy. Fortunately, none of these projects have yet come to fruition, but the threat remains. For example, as a human population grows, it inevitably needs more hydroelectric power and irrigation. Building dams to accomplish this would make the antelope's situation even more precarious. Hunter's antelope also faces threats from livestock competition and drought. The drought in 1984 greatly reduced the numbers of this antelope.

Relocation efforts

Because of the constant threat to its habitat, several attempts have been made to translocate this

Hunter's antelope is one of the many beautiful species of its genus. The continued decline of this species habitat has drastically reduced its population.

antelope. The first of these, however, met with failure. The animals were run down and roped from vehicles in a similar way to a cattle roundup. This severe handling traumatized them and caused many deaths. Afterward the remaining animals were moved to an area considered to be much safer and, after a period of time, turned loose. Unfortunately all the antelope either disappeared or died off for no known reason. It was not discovered until much later that not only was there a problem with the animals, readjusting to a new and totally unfamiliar environment, but their chosen food source was not available. It was simply assumed that Hunter's

antelope ate the long grasses of their native homeland, and similar grasses were available where they were transferred. As it turned out, Hunter's antelope eat the little grasses that grow underneath, and these were totally absent in their new habitat. A population of about 100 was finally established in Tsavo National Park, south of its natural range.

Captive population

Raising captive populations has been attempted twice since World War II. A number of Hunter's antelope were caught, and separate shipments were sent to North America and Europe. In Europe, the animals were placed

in Czechoslovakia at the state zoo, where they had very limited success. Over a period of time, the animals simply died out.

In the United States, relocation met with some early success; however, it was carried out with an extremely narrow gene pool. There were only six animals, and over a period of time the group declined to merely a few survivors. Today this species is listed as critically endangered by IUCN–The World Conservation Union. In the wild it numbers a few hundred to possibly the low thousands and is continuing to decline. There is no healthy captive population existing as a backup against extinction.

Warren D. Thomas

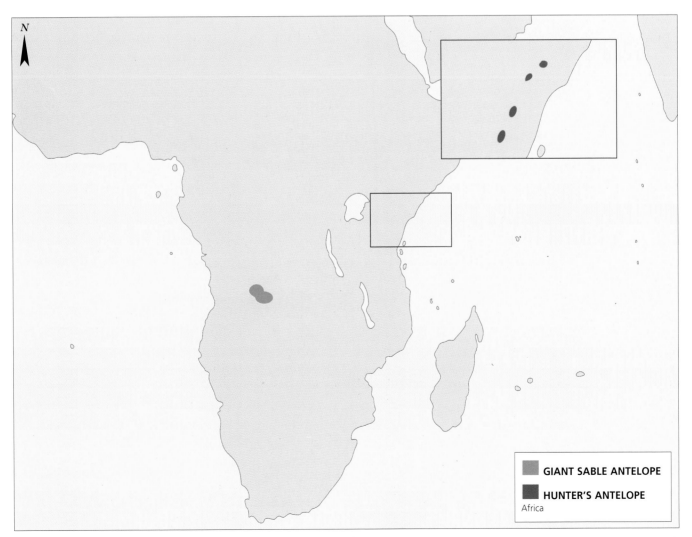

GIANT SABLE ANTELOPE

HUNTER'S ANTELOPE

Africa

Saiga Antelope

(Saiga tartarica)

IUCN: Vulnerable

Weight: 77–152 lb. (35–69 kg)
Shoulder height: 27–32 in.
(70–80 cm)
Diet: Grass, herbs, and leaves
Gestation period: 145 days
Longevity: Males average
about 7 years; females about
12 years
Habitat: Semi-arid steppes or
grasslands
Range: Central Asia; Kirghiz
steppes east to Kazakhstan,
Junggar and west Mongolia

THE SMALL SAIGA antelope has one of the most unusual appearances and life histories of any hoofed animal in the world. It is grayish white and is much lighter in winter than in summer. Females are without horns, but males have buffy yellowish straight ringed horns that are translucent. The average length of the horns is about 9 inches (23 centimeters), but the record is over 16 inches (41 centimeters). The most unusual feature of their appearance is the great bulbous down-turned nose. It is the only hoofed animal to possess a nose of this magnitude in proportion to its body size and configuration. There has long been considerable speculation and argument as to the function of this unusual organ. It is now thought that each nostril sac accomplishes three major functions. It warms the air on inhalation before reaching the lungs, it filters the air of dust and particles, and it moistens the air. All of this makes perfect biological sense for the saiga antelope, because in the winter it lives in an environment that is bitterly cold, very dusty, and extremely dry.

Hardy species

The saiga is a tough little animal, adapted to a hostile environment. It seems to be impervious to heat and cold, and it subsists on forage on which other animals would find difficulty surviving. Their favorite food is wormwood leaves. They can run at speeds of up to 30 miles (50 kilometers) per hour.

Saiga are extremely gregarious and semi-migratory. They are found in herds of 10 to 100,000. The smaller herds join together to form increasingly larger and

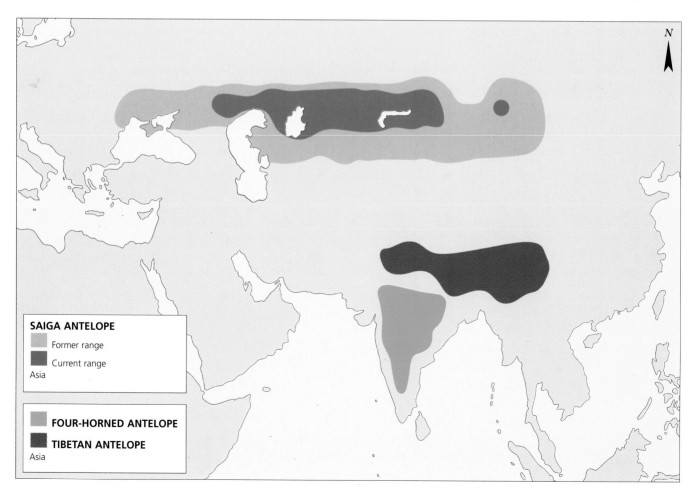

SAIGA ANTELOPE

◻ Former range

◼ Current range

Asia

◼ **FOUR-HORNED ANTELOPE**

◼ **TIBETAN ANTELOPE**

Asia

larger herds in autumn, when they migrate toward slightly warmer areas. With the advent of spring, they return to the colder areas.

There are two subspecies of saiga. The common saiga, *Saiga tartarica tartarica,* is found from the Kirghiz steppes to west Junggar in China. The other subspecies is the Mongolian, *S. tartarica mongolica.* It is found in southwest Mongolia and is considered endangered.

Mating and migrating

One of the most remarkable aspects of the saiga is its unusual method of reproduction. While they are adapted to their environment, they are quite different from most other animals. The males are pugnacious by nature, but during the rutting period they simplify their existence by concentrating on two functions: fighting and breeding. They eat next to nothing and they expend an enormous amount of energy. Their neck swells to almost half again its normal size. Against rival males, they can be quickly lethal with their spikelike horns. The competition is so fierce that only one out of every six breeding-age males actually services the females. After the mating period they migrate, covering ground at a speed of about nine miles (15 kilometers) per hour. They eventually will cover about 930 miles, or 1,500 kilometers. At this point the males are faced with their biggest crisis. In this harsh environment with the bitter cold and dry weather, they are in the worst possible physical condition. Therefore, of the breeding males, less than 5 to 10 percent survive to the next year. Even a high per-

The saiga antelope's prominent feature is its large, down-turned nose. This is thought to be an adaptation to the cold, dusty, and dry conditions that prevail in its Central Asian habitat.

centage of those that did not breed also perish because of the energy expended fighting over females. The future of this species, realistically, is dependent on the next season's calves.

High birth rate

At calving time the females generally have multiple births. Their first birth is usually a single one, but from then on 75 percent of the females have twins and a small percentage bear triplets. Quadruplets have been recorded as well. This is the positive side of the reproductive story. The negative side is that 20 percent of all the calves die in the first month. They are preyed on by wolves and steppe eagles. After the first winter, 40 percent of the calves will have survived. A factor in their favor is that calves are capable of a high degree of independence very soon after birth. They consume grass at four days of age and can outrun a horse at eight days. They are also quick to achieve sexual maturity. About 86 percent of the female calves surviving can successfully mate by the time they are eight months of age. The sum total of this incredible and unusual reproductive drama is that the saiga antelope can average, in a protected area, a 115 percent increase in population in a given year.

The numbers of Tibetan antelope are dwindling due to the illegal poaching of the animal for its prized soft wool, which is used to make shawls known as *shatoosh*. These shawls may be sold for thousands of dollars.

The saiga's history with humans was at one time disastrous. In the aftermath of the Russian revolution, when stability within Russia virtually fell apart, the saiga were afforded little or no protection, and the males especially were destroyed in great numbers. They were killed for their hides and meat, and the males were particularly sought after for their horns, which were important in Asian folk medicine. By 1930 their numbers had diminished to around 1,000 animals. It was then that the Russian government put very strict controls and protection on the remaining population. This included armed patrols with instructions to implement a policy against possible or probable poachers: to shoot first and ask questions later. The remaining saiga population at once started to grow, and from that remaining number, today's population is around 2 million.

Current status

Saiga antelope are still protected by the Russian government, although a quota of about 200,000 a year is permitted. The Mongolian population is still in great jeopardy, numbering only about 600, which is why that subspecies is endangered. Having been contemporary with woolly mammoths and once ranging as far west as Great Britain and as far east as Alaska, this remarkable animal has a very long history and is virtually unchanged today.

If the Mongolian subspecies can be afforded the same quality of protection that the Russian common saiga enjoys, it is likely that it too can demonstrate a dramatic comeback.

Tibetan Antelope

(Pantholops hodgsonii)

IUCN: Vulnerable

Weight: 85–110 lb. (40–52 kg)
Shoulder height: 30–35 in.
(80–90 cm)
Diet: Grasses, herbs, and shrubs
Gestation period: About
180 days
Longevity: No valid record;
probably about 15 years
Habitat: High, dry plateau
grasslands 10,000–16,000 ft.
(3,050–4,880 m)
Range: Sichuan, Ladakh,
Xizang (Tibet, Qinghai plateau)

THE TIBETAN ANTELOPE is a high-altitude animal that is found in a very demanding environment. Like so many other animals in exacting environments, it is well equipped to meet the challenge. It is more closely related to the caprids (sheep and goats) than to true antelopes. Its coat is dense and woolly. In summer it is a reddish fawn to light gray color, and in some cases it is brownish with white underparts. In winter, the breeding season, the face and the front of the mature male's legs are black. This dark color curves over the shoulder from the legs back to a rump patch. The rest of the fur is light gray to tan with white underparts. In winter the females are fawn to russet and may show white around the muzzle.

Tibetan antelope live singly or in small groups of four or five. These groups coalesce into groups of over 2,000 animals toward the time of migration.

The antelope migrate twice a year, following the seasons and the available grass. Oddly enough, the males migrate separately from the females. They are most active at dawn and dusk.

The rutting season is in October, and the young are born in the spring. The females have two nipples and generally have one or two offspring. There is a high mortality rate among the young due to eagles, wolves, and other predators.

The males possess spectacular horns for their size, averaging 20 inches (50 centimeters). The longest horns recorded were 28 inches (70 centimeters). On first encounter, the horns appear to be relatively straight, but there is a slight curve backward, with the points curving forward. There are about 15 or 20 ridges along two-thirds of their length, and they are dark in color. These animals have a large air sac in their nostrils that preheats the air and helps filter the dust. When excited or frightened, they can run up to 50 miles per hour (80 kilometers per hour).

Little has been known until recently about this antelope, but the available knowledge has been enhanced by recent studies conducted by George Schaller (author of *Wildlife of the Tibetan Steppe*, University of Chicago Press, 1998) of the Wildlife Conservation Society (New York Zoological Society).

Killed for fashion

Tibetan antelope live in an area where there are few humans, but their contacts with the small human population have contributed to their decline. The males are sought for their horns, which are used in folk medicine. Both the males and females are highly sought after for their pelts, from which wool is derived. The wool is known as *shatoosh* and is referred to as the king of the wools as it has an extremely fine texture. Until recent years, shawls made from *shatoosh* were often available in fine shops in New York, London, and Paris for between $2,500 and $8,000 apiece. *Shatoosh* are still sometimes imported illegally. Each shawl represents the death of five Tibetan antelope.

Tibetan antelope are presently protected over their whole range, but implementation of this protection is not very effective. There have been some efforts to cut off the flow of *shatoosh*. In 1992, the government of India confiscated the wool of 13,000 Tibetan antelope. The antelope is listed in Appendix 1 of the Convention on International Trade in Endangered Species of Wild Fauna and Flora (CITES), which means it is subject to an international trade ban.

The total population has dropped from 3 million in the 1950s to between 65,000 and 72,000 animals. Without more rigorous enforcement, the pressure of poaching for their pelts and horns affects their stability and makes their future uncertain.

The Tibetan antelope has occasionally been kept in captivity by chance pickups by indigenous people with little success. Due to the antelopes isolated range, there has never been a major effort to capture them for propagation in zoos. It is unknown what the level of success could be.

Warren D. Thomas

ANTS

Class: Insecta

Order: Hymenoptera

Family: Formicidae

Ants have been crawling around on the earth since at least the Mesozoic era, or for about the last 80 million years. Currently ants live in almost all terrestrial environments and are among the dominant organisms of the world. A single acre (approximately 0.4 hectare) of soil in the Amazonian rain forest may contain more than three million ants.

It is estimated that all social insects, including ants, termites, bees, and wasps, comprise slightly more than 75 percent of the total insect population of the world. In tropical regions, several hundred different ant species may live within a single square mile (2.6 square kilometers).

Ants are related to bees and wasps and belong to the insect family Formicidae. The family name is based on the fact that many ants produce formic acid, which protects them from natural enemies.

In general, ants are predators of insects and other small invertebrates, but they also act as herbivores (plant feeders) and granivores (seed feeders). Ants alter their environment by moving soil about in an activity similar to that of earthworms. Many plants benefit from this effort because it aids in seed dispersal and aerates the soil.

Like all insects, ants have three main body regions: head, thorax, and abdomen. Three pairs of legs are attached to the thorax. Although there is considerable variation in body forms among different ant species, the head is often rectangular and wider than the thorax, while the abdomen is usually large and egg-shaped. The color of adults is most often black, brown, or red. They range in length from 0.1 to 25.4 millimeters.

All ants are social insects, living in colonies that contain three castes: queens, males, and workers. These castes differ in size, appearance, and function. Workers are sterile, wingless females that make up most of the colony—those commonly seen at picnics or in the home. Queens are larger than those in the other castes and are usually winged, although their wings are shed soon after mating. A queen starts an ant colony and lays most of the eggs. Males are winged and short-lived: they die soon after mating. During a particular season of the year, winged males and queens engage in mating flights.

Ants make up from 10 to 15 percent of the animal population in most terrestrial environments. Yet ants, like other organisms, have their rare or locally distributed species. In such groups, population extinction rates tend to be highest. Thus, it is not surprising that several of the 8,800 living species of ants are considered to be threatened or rare.

Research entomologists have demonstrated that some rare species of ants use conservation methods to reduce their chance of extinction. Some species have multiple queens instead of only one. The cave-inhabiting population of *Erebomyrma urichi* that occupied Trinidad's Oropouche Cave in 1961 was estimated not to exceed 400 individuals. This species had multiple queens. Other species engage in mating among members of the same colony, in contrast to the outbreeding between colonies of more common species.

Various rare species of ants can be grouped under three ecological categories: bog endemics, cave-inhabiting (troglophic), and parasitic species. Among the known bog endemics are *Formica*

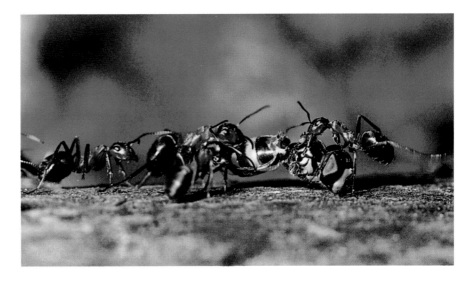

These red ants are transporting a hoverfly (family Syrphidae) to help feed their colony.

neorufibarbis, Lasius minutus, L. speculiventris, and *Leptothorax muscorum*. The population of *Lasius minutus* at Hidden Lake, Michigan, nested in 700 mounds in the 1950s. Since one colony occupies an average of about 4.4 mounds, the population of the species was about 160 colonies.

The parasitic species are social parasites on other ants, and they are rare. A threatened species, *Manica parasitica*, is recorded only from nests of *M. bradleyi* at the top of Pollydome in Yosemite National Park, California. A second population was discovered in the Stanislaus National Forest of California. Another threatened species, the social parasite *Teleutomyrmex schneideri*, has a limited population on the east side of the Saas-Fee Valley of Switzerland. It was found only in a specific elevation range. Another population was found in the French Alps.

In several European countries, numerous species of wood ants (*Formica*) have been recognized as near threatened. These ants are voracious predators that help to control various pest insects. Loss and alteration of habitats is resulting in a rapid decline of many species of ants.

Thomas C. Emmel and
Richard A. Arnold

Giant Armadillo

(Priodontes maximus)

ESA: Endangered

IUCN: Endangered

Class: Mammalia
Order: Xenarthra
Family: Dasypodidae
Weight: 90–130 lb. (40–60 kg)
Head-body length: 30–40 in. (75–100 cm)
Diet: Mostly termites and ants
Gestation period: 120 days
Longevity: 12–15 years
Habitat: Savanna, thorn forest, and tropical forest
Range: East of the Andes from northwest Venezuela to northeast Argentina

THE GIANT ARMADILLO, like the other 19 species in the family Dasypodidae, is easily recognized by its body armor. It is quickly distinguished from the other species by its large size; the next largest armadillo is roughly only half as large. Another distinguishing characteristic of the giant armadillo is its possession of up to 100 small, unenameled, peg-like teeth, which are shed as the animal ages. Once common in its preferred habitats east of the Andes mountain range, the giant armadillo—like all armadillos except the nine-banded species—appears to be on the decline.

A little tank

Looking like a small tank as it ambles along, it is easy to see why this animal was given the name armadillo, Spanish for "little armored one." The skin on the upper surface of the back, head, and tail, as well as on the sides and outer surface of the limbs, is modified into a series of horn-like plates. Those on the back and sides are very thick. Eleven to thirteen of the rows of plates on the back, as well as three to four rows at the neck, are separated by areas of flexible skin, which allow the animal to flex its body. This thick armor on the back and sides forms a carapace which hangs down, helping to protect the limbs and soft underparts. The armor, which can comprise as much as 20 percent of total body weight, shields the armadillo from predators while allowing it to move about with relative ease.

The armadillo's front limbs are short but extremely powerful and equipped with thick, hook-like claws, the third being very large. These forelegs serve the armadillo well, as it is a prodigious digger when it is in search of its primary food source of termites and ants. Studies carried out in 1985 showed that ants comprised up to 78 percent of its diet. Armadillos are reported to also eat other insects, along with occasional spiders, worms, snakes, and carrion.

Because the giant armadillo is reluctant to be far from protective shelter at any time, it digs new burrows with every expansion of its territory. These burrows are most often located in active termite mounds. Although the giant armadillo is traditionally thought to occur mostly in undisturbed tropical forests, it was discovered that more than 90 percent of giant armadillo burrows in Brazil are found in grassland and brushland.

Highly tuned senses
In addition to possessing good vision and hearing, the giant armadillo has a well-developed olfactory area of the brain. All of its senses must serve the armadillo well if it should be stalked by a predator.

Because the giant armadillo cannot completely enclose itself in its carapace like some other armadillo species, it must rely on

The giant armadillo is twice the size of other armadillos and is covered with body armor. Unfortunately, its great size and protective carapace have not helped protect it from being hunted for its skin and persecuted by humans throughout its range.

detecting danger early to allow time to dig itself in.

Armadillos are solitary creatures; they are rarely observed together except when mating. Gestation takes roughly four months and results in the birth of one or occasionally two young. At birth the young weigh approximately 4 ounces (113 grams), and are covered with soft, leathery skin that hardens in a few days. They are weaned at four to six weeks and become sexually mature at 9 to 12 months.

Victims of persecution
Like many other mammals in South America, giant armadillos are increasingly becoming casualties of the agriculture and timber industries. Many South American farmers have been known to persecute and attack armadillos for the damage done to cultivated fields by their extensive networks of dens. In many areas they are killed for their armored skin. The unusual skins are then turned into a variety of containers and handcrafted objects. Sometimes armadillos are cooked and eaten as a delicacy.

The armadillo is also persecuted by humans because of a superstition that the animal is a graveyard demon that digs up graves and eats the remains. If this unusual animal is to survive, a program of education is necessary to counter hostility and persecution.

Terry Tompkins

N

GIANT ARMADILLO
South America

Artemisia Granatensis

IUCN: Endangered

Family: Asteraceae
Habitat: Mountain ranges
Range: Andalucia, Spain

ARTEMISIA GRANATENSIS is a perennial herbaceous plant, known in Spain as *manzanilla real*. It is a very rare species of the daisy family. The plant is endemic to the Sierra Nevada of Andalucia. The total population of about 1,000 individual plants grows at an altitude of over 8,200 feet (2,500 meters) on the peaks of Veleta, Mulhacén, Caballo, Alcazaba and Chullo in the Sierra Nevada Nature Park. Collection of plants from the wild has been the main threat to this species.

There are about 300 species of *Artemisia* that grow wild in northern temperate parts of the world, western parts of South America, and southern Africa. Some of the species are grown as garden plants because they have pretty, finely divided silvery leaves. The genus also includes medicinal plants such as the wormwoods, which include some of the most bitter herbs known. The essential oil of one species of *Artemisia* was used to make the alcoholic aperitif absinthe. Consumption of this drink caused serious problems in Europe and the United States in the 19th century. Symptoms included hallucinations, mental deterioration, and sterility, and caused absinthe to be banned in many countries. Other species are used in perfumery, food flavoring, and as a cure for a wide range of illnesses.

The use of wild *Artemisia* has been a significant threat to some species, and 48 species and varieties are currently listed in the IUCN Red List of Threatened Plants. About a third of these occur in North America, includ-

The Sierra Nevada mountains in Andalucia, Spain, are the home of *Artemisia granatensis*. Despite the elevation, people still collect the plant.

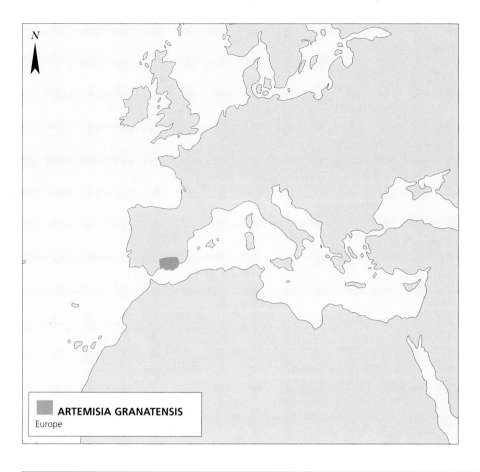

ing a subspecies of *Artemisia tilesii* that has properties similar to codeine and is used by some Native Americans. In Europe, 14 species and varieties of *Artemisia* are threatened.

Artemisia granatensis has been used medicinally for several centuries, and is drunk as an infusion (the leaves are soaked in water to extract their properties). The species is protected by Spanish law, by the EU Directive, and by the Bern Convention (Annex 1). Strict protection in its natural habitat is essential for its survival. The Cordoba Botanic Garden plays an important role in conserving the species. Tissue culture techniques have been used to propagate plants that can be returned to the wild.

Sara Oldfield

Asper

(Zingel asper)

IUCN: Critically endangered

Class: Actinopterygii
Order: Perciformes
Family: Percidae
Length: 6 in. (15 cm)
Reproduction: Egg layer
Habitat: Shallow and fast streams
Range: Rhone River basin, France and Switzerland

AS A MEMBER OF the clan called European strebers and a close relative of the critically endangered asprete (*Romanichthys valsanicola*), the asper has been subjected to many kinds of environmental pressures. Pollution and degradation of river habitat have drastically reduced the range of this fish, which probably always existed in low numbers and is now on the verge of extinction. Soil erosion is particularly destructive, because it produces too much silt in the water. Aspers lay their eggs on the river bottom and depend on silt-free rocks and gravel to prevent them from being smothered.

Isolated populations

Changes in the speed of river currents due to human-made modifications to the flow of the Rhone have contributed to the decline of this species. The asper is found within the Rhone River system of southern France, but populations are becoming isolated. Small isolated populations are also found in Switzerland. The asper is now found in only approximately 17 percent of the range that it occupied at the beginning of the 20th century. As human urban and agricultural activities continue to intensify in the region, the future of the asper is at best uncertain.

The asper is the smallest of three European strebers. The other two species are the streber (*Zingel streber*) and the zingel

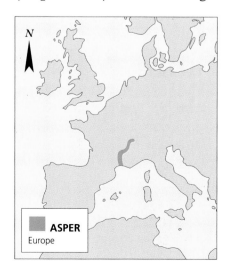

(*Z. zingel*), both of which are vulnerable. The asper is 6-inches (15-centimeters) long and has a slender, tapered body and a mouth that is low on the snout, allowing it to pick up insects, small fish, and fish eggs from the river bottom. It has two dorsal fins, a spiny fin toward the front for protection from predators, and a soft fin toward the tail. Most of the body, as well as the gill covers, is generously scaled as a defense against abrasive river conditions. Coloration varies, generally with several large, dark, saddle-like patches on the back over a brown background and yellowish sides and belly. There is a prominent dark vertical band at the base of the tail, and the sides often exhibit several vertical bands as well. The shy asper uses this camouflage to hide among river rocks during the day; observations indicate that this species is most active at night.

Adapted to its environment

The asper has a special adaptation that allows it to exist more easily in its river environment. Unlike many other fish such as minnows and salmonids, which use the water column for feeding and other activities, the asper has no swim bladder—a sac that fills with gas to regulates a fish's buoyancy. In a river environment, fish that stay on the bottom of the river benefit by having no swim bladder, so they are less buoyant. They sink to the bottom of the river and consequently do not have to swim as much in order to maintain their position.

The asper has a particularly low reproductive rate for a fish of the perch family. It is a spring-spawning fish that lays adhesive eggs within the stones and rocks of the river bottom; a single female can lay as many as 5,000 eggs. After an incubation period of up to two weeks, the eggs hatch. Newly hatched fish feed on their yolk sac until they begin taking their first food—usually microscopic river plankton.

William E. Manci

Asprete

(Romanichthys valsanicola)

IUCN: Critically endangered

Class: Actinopterygii
Order: Perciformes
Family: Percidae
Length: 5 in. (13 cm)
Reproduction: Egg layer
Habitat: Fast-flowing streams
Range: Vâlsan River, Romania

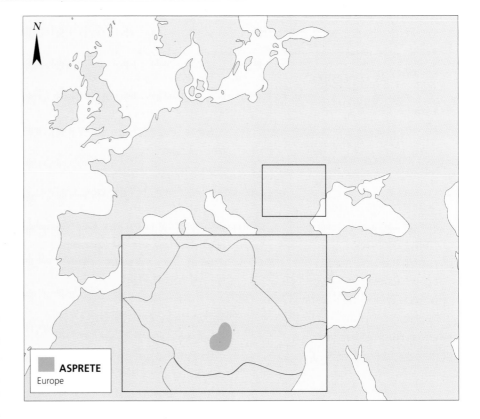

ASPRETE
Europe

WHILE IT ONCE occupied four tributary rivers of the Danube River basin in eastern Europe, the asprete is now confined to a single tributary: the Vâlsan River in Romania. Years of abusive pollution and disregard for wildlife have decimated populations of this fish. Literally poisoned and smothered in its home, the asprete faces an uphill struggle to avoid extinction. During the Communist era in eastern Europe, government officials promoted commercial and industrial development with little or no concern for the environment. As a result, the land was systematically stripped of its vegetation and the air and water were poisoned with industrial pollutants. This activity either killed asprete populations directly or left spawning areas filled with silt, making them unusable for reproductive purposes.

As a river fish, the asprete has an uncommon adaptation that allows it to deal with its river environment. To prevent being forced downstream by strong currents, the asprete has no swim bladder—a sac that fills with gas that is used to regulate buoyancy. However, in a river environment, benthic species—ones that stay on the bottom—lack a swim bladder. This allows the asprete to sink to the bottom of the river where it is not forced to swim as much to maintain its position.

Locally, this fish is called the Romanian bullhead perch, but it bears little resemblance to the North American bullhead or other catfish-like species. It does, however, resemble the North American yellow perch, *Perca flavescens*; Europe's asper, *Zingel asper*, also endangered; and Europe's streber, *Z. streber*, and is included in the same family, Percidae. The asprete has the same thin and narrow body, and the back displays two dorsal fins: a short, protective spiny fin in the front, and a longer soft fin directly behind it. Like that of suckers and other bottom feeders, the mouth is low on the snout and is used to catch insects and small fishes. The body is brown on the back and sides with a lighter chin, throat, and belly.

Several dark vertical bars mark the sides, and the pectoral and pelvic fins (just behind the gills and tail) are banded with narrow, dark stripes. The body is heavily scaled, but the head and gill covers are not.

Habits
Biologists believe the asprete is primarily nocturnal (most active at night). It breeds in the spring and hides its adhesive eggs among bottom gravel for protection against predators. During this period both sexes develop nodule-like tubercles on their bodies and fins as a visual indication of their readiness to spawn.

William E. Manci

ASSES

Class: Mammalia

Order: Perissodactyla

Family: Equidae

Subgenus: Equus

Zebras, horses, and asses belong to the same genus, *Equus*, whose most distinctive feature is the foot. The weight of the body is placed on the hoof, and the sole or heel of the foot never touches the ground. This adaptation makes the equine species well suited for running.

Asses were domesticated in the Middle East probably around 4000 B.C.E. Wild asses probably escaped from domesticated groups of animals thousands of years ago, and thus survive in many areas where they had been transplanted by humans. All of the species have highly fragmented populations, and the horse family is one of the most threatened among animals.

African Wild Ass
(Equus africanus sp.)

ESA: Endangered

IUCN: Critically endangered

Weight: 550–640 lb. (250–290 kg)
Shoulder height: 50–57 in. (125–145 cm)
Diet: Grasses, leaves, twigs
Gestation period: 340–365 days
Longevity: 20–30 years
Habitat: Scrub desert
Range: Ethiopia, Somalia, and Sudan

THE HORSE FAMILY is represented in Africa by the wild ass and zebra. The African wild ass has always been confined to the northern and northeast portions of Africa. It persists today in some of the most desolate portions of Ethiopia, Somalia, and possibly Sudan. These areas vary in topography from scrub desert to true desert salt plains with sparse vegetation. These environments are hostile for any creature, yet the wild ass still persists there. Its resilience indicates what a hardy animal it is when not persecuted by humans.

African wild asses eat whatever vegetation they can find. This includes leaves, grasses, and twigs. They drink water whenever it is available and, given the opportunity, will stay relatively close to a source of water. However, they also have the ability to survive for two to three days without drinking.

Two subspecies
There are actually two forms of the African wild ass. The northern form (*Equus africanus africanus*), also known as the Nubian wild ass, is slate gray with a broad, dark stripe down its

back, a cross stripe over the withers, and a dark brush on the end of its tail. Its numbers are few and it is unclear whether it still survives. There are no true Nubian wild asses in captivity. Those that are sometimes called wild asses are suspected of being hybrids—part ass, part donkey.

The southern form of African wild ass is the Somali wild ass (*E. africanus somaliensis*). It is more numerous, but only when compared to its nearly extinct Nubian relative. Otherwise, it is still endangered. In appearance, the Somali wild ass differs from the Nubian by being slightly larger, with heavy neck muscles, a short dark mane, a white ring around its muzzle, and a dark stripe down its back. It usually lacks the cross stripe over the withers, but has very distinctive horizontal striping around the lower legs, both front and rear. It also has a dark brush on the end of its tail.

A hardy species

Most of these wild asses, particularly the Somali wild ass, were relatively safe until recent times simply because they lived in areas hostile to humans. Daytime temperatures in their habitat can soar up to 130 degrees Fahrenheit (54 degrees Centigrade), while nighttime temperatures can drop to freezing. Water is scarce. In the past, the only people who traveled through these areas were occasional cattle trains of nomadic wanderers carrying primitive weapons. So the num-

The African wild ass can survive for two to three days without water and can live in hostile environments with temperatures of up to 130 degrees Fahrenheit (54 degrees Centigrade).

Onagers (*Equus hemionus onager*), or Persian wild asses, survive in northern Iran. While they flee from predators, they are not afraid to fight among themselves.

ber of animals taken was negligible. However, with increasing human populations, people have been forced to take their goats and sheep into more inhospitable areas such as the habitat of the Somali ass, competing for what little vegetation there is. Better weapons have made poaching simpler and more efficient. Finally, both Somalia and Ethiopia have been the sites of civil war. Armed combat always takes its toll on wildlife.

Captive populations

The Somali wild ass has a captive population of more than 70 individuals. Animals were imported and successful populations set up first in Europe and later in Israel. In captivity the Somali wild ass has shown some promise. If the wild population were lost, these captive populations could be used to reintroduce the animal into the wild.

Asian Wild Ass

(Equus hemionus sp.*)*

ESA: Endangered

IUCN: Vulnerable

Weight: 550–640 lb.
(250–290 kg)
Shoulder height: 45–55 in.
(115–140 cm)
Diet: Grasses, leaves, twigs
Gestation period: 330–370 days
Longevity: 20–25 years (30 years in captivity)
Habitat: Grasslands to desert
Range: Central Asia, northwest India, western Pakistan

THE HORSE FAMILY was once well represented in Europe and Asia by a number of wild asses and two true horses: the tarpan, now extinct, and Przewalski's horse (*Equus przewalskii*), which still survives. Two of the asses are also extinct, but several subspecies of Asian wild asses survive. The Asiatic wild ass (*E. hemionus hemionus*) is found in southern

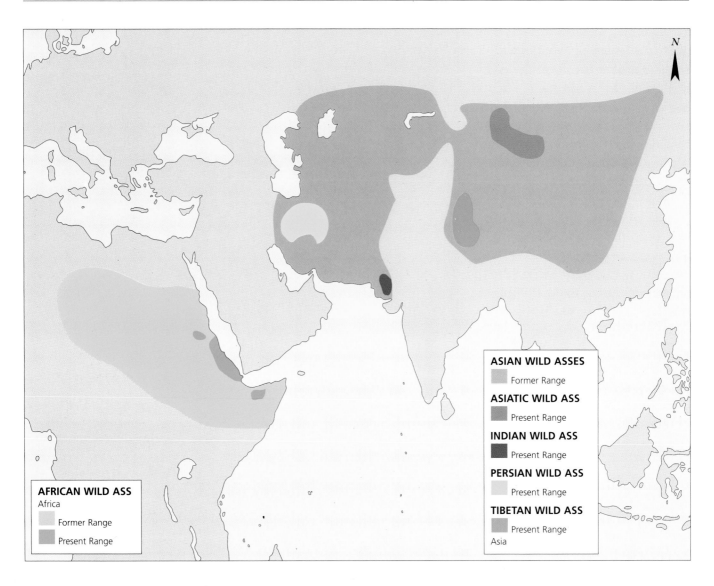

ASIAN WILD ASSES
Former Range

ASIATIC WILD ASS
Present Range

INDIAN WILD ASS
Present Range

PERSIAN WILD ASS
Present Range

TIBETAN WILD ASS
Present Range
Asia

AFRICAN WILD ASS
Africa

Former Range

Present Range

Mongolia and western China in the autonomous region Zinjiang Uygur. Wild asses are usually found on the steppe or open grasslands. Sometimes they are found on hilly terrain, but this is not common.

Wild ass predators

The asses are primarily grass eaters. They rely on their keen senses of sight, hearing, and smell and their ability to run to escape danger. In the areas in which they live, wild asses can see for miles, and it is very difficult for a predator to approach them without being seen. Before many of their natural predators were killed off, wild asses were preyed upon in some areas by wolves and occasionally tigers. But now that these carnivores have been eliminated, the wild asses' primary predator is human.

Encroachment by people has been the severest threat to their population. Camels, horses, donkeys, goats, and sheep belonging to nomadic herdspeople destroy a lot of the prime grazing areas that were formerly the exclusive domain of wild asses.

Impure bloodlines

Another problem that has contributed to the slow decline of the Asian wild ass is hybridization. When domestic horses and donkeys come in contact with wild asses they interbreed with them, resulting in hybrid asses that destroy the pure bloodline.

Over much of their range wild asses are protected. However, that protection is not always enforced to any great degree.

Subspecies

The onager or Persian wild ass (*E. hemionus onager*) has been introduced into Israel, and numbers there are increasing. The populations in Iran seem to be stable. The Asiatic and Persian

The distinctive striping around the lower legs of the Somali ass, together with its light buffy color, makes it an unusually handsome species.

wild asses are very similar in size. The largest of the wild asses, *E. hemionus kiang*, is known simply as the kiang or Tibetan wild ass. It inhabits grassy areas but has never been found in large numbers, and its total population is now severely reduced. The Chinese government has yet to give this species strong protection.

Aggressive defense

The Tibetan wild ass is an animal that, like all of the wild asses, will defend itself by kicking, biting, and striking. It can be formidable when trapped but is easy prey for human hunters with guns.

The Indian wild ass (*E. hemionus khur*) occurs in northwest India and Pakistan in a desolate area known as the Rann of Kutch—an area where intense sunlight beats down on a salt plain. It is an extremely severe habitat with soaring temperatures. The Indian wild ass, however, survives by living in and around the more hospitable boundaries of the rann.

During recent times, the Indian wild ass population has been decimated. Even with protection, its numbers are probably less than 400 to 500. Prospects for its long-term survival do not look good. A few individuals live in captivity in Indian zoos, but they have not flourished.

Unpopular animals

One problem the wild asses have faced in captivity is that they have not been popular. They are not very spectacular looking—with the exception of the kiang, which is beautifully colored. The rest are dun-colored or gray. Because the wild asses are not crowd pleasers, zoos having limited space often devote that space to an animal that is perhaps just as endangered but much showier.

Warren D. Thomas

Ribbon-tailed Astrapia

(Astrapia mayeri)

IUCN: Vulnerable

Class: Aves
Order: Passeriformes
Family: Paradisaeidae
Length: Males, about 10 in. (25 cm) long with a 3-ft. (0.9-m) tail; females have a less elaborate tail
Weight: Unknown
Clutch size: Probably 1–2 eggs
Incubation: Unknown
Diet: Probably mostly fruits and seeds, some invertebrates and small vertebrates such as frogs or lizards
Habitat: Forests
Range: East-central highlands of New Guinea

SPLENDIDLY COLORED with elaborate ornamental plumage, birds of paradise qualify as the world's most spectacular birds. They have fascinated people for thousands of years, and indigenous peoples have long prized the ornate feathers unique to each species. As Europeans began exploring islands of the western Pacific, birds of paradise became known to the entire world. Then, as the market for novelty feathers in the fashion industry expanded, hunting for bird-of-paradise plumage grew. Before long, ornithologists wanted to know more about these unusual birds.

Crow relatives

Some early researchers suggested that an African or Asian starling species may have been the original stock from which the birds of paradise developed. However, birds of paradise share many features with crows and jays, and many species are regularly described as being jay-like. The stronger argument favors birds of paradise originating from a crowlike ancestor that became isolated on New Guinea. A rugged island with tall mountains and dense forests, New Guinea provided many opportunities for birds of paradise to adapt to special conditions. Thus, most species are found in particular forest types at specific elevations. Of the 45 species, most are confined to New Guinea. A few species have adapted to nearby islands and northern Australia.

Recently described

The ribbon-tailed astrapia was the last bird of paradise to be described as a species. The first published mention of the bird appeared in a 1936 book called *Papuan Wonderland*. The entry was brief and made no effort to identify the birds in question as a new species. Two years later, Fred Shaw Mayer, who spent three decades exploring and collecting natural history specimens in New Guinea, sent two tail feathers to the British Museum of Natural History in London. On the basis of those two feathers, the species was described for science in 1939.

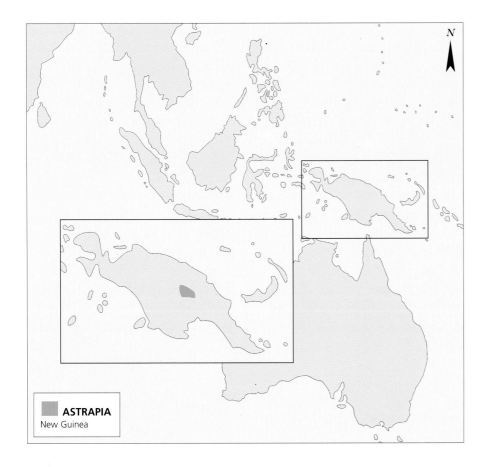

ASTRAPIA
New Guinea

Appearance

The male of this species has a black back that has a bronze to green iridescence; much of the head, throat, and upper breast are an iridescent yellow-green with some purple showing on the upper breast and throat. From the cheeks to the back of the head is a shiny violet to purple. The tail is 3 feet (0.9 meter) long and is black except for a central pair of feathers that are white with black tips. The female is less spectacular than the male, with a blue-black back that fades to brown-black at the rump. The head and upper neck are black with a green-blue iridescence; the breast and belly are light brown to rufous and strongly barred with black; the wings and tail are brown except for central tail feathers that have white bases. The beak is black, and the feet and toes are dark gray.

Tree dweller

Very few details are known about the ribbon-tailed astrapia. Apparently it spends much time in the lower canopy, or mid-level, of tall forest trees. Whether it prefers certain tree types over others is not clear, but the arboreal lifestyle suits this bird. Its long, thin central tail feathers would probably wear out quickly if dragged along the ground. These feathers are crucial to the bird's reproductive cycle.

Mating among birds usually entails a courtship of some sort during which the male and female attract each other. Courtship behaviors can be highly ritualized and are always distinct because they help males and females recognize their own species. Birds of paradise are largely, but not exclusively, polygynous—that is, males mate with more than one female.

Those species in which the males and females are quite similar are usually monogamous (one male mates with one female). Those species with drastic differences between the genders are usually polygynous. In all five astrapia species, the females differ markedly from the males and are therefore probably polygynous. Typically, the polygynous birds of paradise develop traditional arenas where males gather to display themselves. These areas are almost always in larger forest trees with many bare, horizontal lower branches on which a male can perform and be clearly seen. Visibility is extremely important, as the elaborate feathers of the birds of paradise are there to attract females. Depending on the species, the male exhibits a variety of wing spreading, tail flaring, and crest erecting. The display also includes a call that is unique to the species. With some species, several males may use one tree. In other species, single males display in a single tree.

Separate lives

After mating, the females of polygynous species leave to build their nests and raise their young alone. The males continue displaying for as long as females respond but do nothing to help with rearing young. For many species the males live entirely apart from the females except for this brief courtship period.

A captive male ribbon-tailed astrapia has been seen to react to a female by posturing sideways to her, cocking his head, first drooping his wings then raising them over his back, and vigorously shaking his long tail, all the while emitting a guttural sound.

Specific information about nest building, brood size, incubation period, nestling period, fledgling behavior, replacement broods, age at first breeding, and longevity are not known. The few nests that have been described were all made of small vines and rootlets of plants growing in trees. Where the nests were placed by the birds has not been recorded; presumably, they build on horizontal branches well off the forest floor. Long tails would be a handicap for a cavity-nesting species; and even the females have long tails, although not as long as those of the males.

Remarkable survival

Protecting a species vulnerable to human enterprise is very difficult when so little is known about its natural history. Apparently, the ribbon-tailed astrapia survived hundreds of years of plume hunting, particularly the intense years between the 1880s and the beginning of the 20th century, when millions of birds of paradise were killed for the plume market. Despite the pressure, they survived.

One explanation is that the marketplace handled only adult male plumage, which birds may require five years to acquire.

Young males with less than full plumage are known to have bred, allowing the species to continue without some of its male members. The ribbon-tailed astrapia also occupies a remote mountain habitat that was inconvenient for plume hunters to reach. This isolation probably saved it, for its population cannot be large in such a small island habitat. Although legally protected, the ribbon-tailed astrapia could become quickly jeopardized by human activities such as mining, agriculture, or timber cutting for lumber or firewood.

Kevin Cook

Aye-Aye
(Daubentonia madagascariensis)

| **ESA:** Endangered |
| **IUCN:** Endangered |

Class: Mammalia
Order: Primates
Family: Daubentoniidae
Weight: 4½–6½ lb. (2–3 kg)
Length: 40 in. (100 cm), including tail
Diet: Fruit, especially coconuts; insect larvae
Gestation period: Unknown
Longevity: Unknown
Habitat: Tropical forests, mangrove swamps, cultivated areas
Range: Northern and eastern Madagascar, Nosy Mangabe Island

THE AYE-AYE IS THE only surviving representative of its family. Its closest relatives, which were larger, died out several centuries

ago. The aye-aye has an unusual appearance for a primate, and at first it was thought to be a squirrel because of its rodent-like front teeth. However, a German zoologist named Schreber classified it as a lemur in 1775; lemurs belong to the order Primates. It was not until the mid-1800s when the English naturalist Richard Owen closely studied its teeth that the aye-aye was recognized as a different kind of primate.

Unusual primate

The aye-aye has no close living relatives. It resembles the lemurs but, in addition, it has certain features similar to those of various extinct primates. The aye-aye has opposable thumbs, which it can place beside other digits as people can; a flat nail on its big toe; and specific skull features. These combine to classify the aye-aye as a modern primate, although an unusual one.

Aye-ayes have claws on all their fingers and toes except for the big toe. They are nocturnal

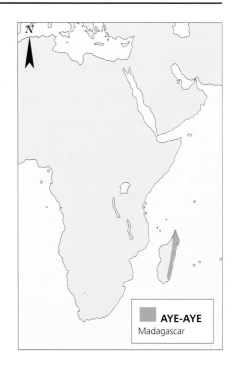

AYE-AYE
Madagascar

and feed mostly on fruit and beetle grubs, but not on larger insects. They have several notable adaptations related to their diet. First, the middle finger is thin, almost wiry, and is used like a probe to pull grubs out from beneath bark and to scoop coconut flesh through a hole in the shell. The aye-aye will creep along branches of old trees at night, gently tapping the wood with its middle finger as it listens with its large, naked ears for a change in tone that indicates the presence of a hollow where a grub may be lurking.

Long incisors

The aye-aye has only a single pair of incisors in each jaw. These grow long and continuously in much the same way as those of a rodent, so its teeth remain sharp for gnawing on branches and cutting leafy twigs for nest building.

The aye-aye also uses its long middle finger for sweeping water into its mouth (at 40 strokes per minute), combing its fur, scratching, and picking its teeth.

Although it is about the same size as a lemur, the aye-aye looks larger because of its fur, which consists of long, coarse, blackish brown hairs overlying a denser layer of very short white hair. It has a long bushy tail and large eyes specially adapted for night vision. Its pointed nose gives it a foxlike appearance. Usually the aye-aye remains silent, but occasionally it gives out a short cry that has been compared to the sound of two pieces of metal being rubbed together.

Arboreal

Aye-ayes are quadrupedal, meaning that when they are on the ground they leap around on all fours. It is their claws that make them such agile tree climbers. For the most part they are arboreal, living in trees. They spend the day asleep, curled up in a ball and resting—either in a nest of leaves, twigs, and branches or in the hollows of trees.

At night aye-ayes move around either singly or in pairs.

Little is known about their breeding behavior, but it is believed that a single infant is born and reared during the months of February and March. Aye-ayes are born in a spherical nest about 20 inches (51 centimeters) in diameter, with a single entrance. The nest doubles as a nursery for the first year of the baby's life. The aye-aye has a single pair of nipples, situated on the abdomen.

The aye-aye is sparsely distributed in the forests of east,

The aye-aye has a pointed nose that gives it an almost foxlike appearance. It is very agile and has strong claws that make it an excellent climber.

north, and northwest Madagascar. Its population is unknown, but it is highly elusive and greatly threatened by habitat destruction. It appears adaptable in its choice of habitat and can be found in primary rain forest, deciduous forest, secondary forest, cultivated areas, dry scrub forest, and possibly mangrove swamps. It is thought that the aye-aye needs tall, mature trees in which to build its nests. However, two of the trees it uses for nesting and as a food source are also cut for construction and cleared for agriculture.

Sign of misfortune

Because it is surprisingly fearless around humans, the aye-aye is easy to capture. Unfortunately for the aye-aye, in some areas of Madagascar it is regarded as a signal of misfortune and killed on sight. Many inhabitants of the island regard the aye-aye with dread, believing that one touch from it can cause death. Legend

also credits it with being a reincarnation of long dead ancestors. By 1933 the aye-aye was thought to be extinct, but it was rediscovered in 1957 by J. J. Petter. By 1966 it was estimated that there were less than a dozen aye-ayes left, and the island of Nosy Mangabe—just off the coast of Madagascar—was declared a reserve for these remaining few. Although they were transferred to the island, by 1976 there were apparently only two or three left.

Remarkable survival

The continued survival of the aye-aye in the face of its many problems is a tribute to the tenacity of this rare primate.

Many species persist in spite of challenges brought on by human encroachment, but sooner or later there is no escape.

In 1994 forty individuals were counted in captivity, with some successful breeding. The aye-aye is still present in certain areas of Madagascar, where it is protected by law. However, these laws require better enforcement. Unlike some endangered primates, the aye-aye is relatively adaptable, allowing it a better chance of survival in close proximity to human settlements. Nevertheless, its future is in serious jeopardy because of its alarmingly small population.

Sarah Dart

BABBLERS

Class: Aves

Order: Passeriformes

Family: Muscicapidae

Subfamily: Timaliinae

Babblers comprise a diverse group of small songbirds that show some similarities to thrushes and Old World flycatchers. They are an Old World group with 233 species spread across the southern two-thirds of Africa, through southern Asia, and into the islands of Indonesia, the Philippines, and New Guinea. The greatest abundance occurs from India eastward into Indonesia. Most babblers inhabit forests, although a few are truly arboreal. Strong legs and feet suit them for life on the ground. Highly sociable, they often move in flocks of several species together. Small groups frequently engage in mutual preening, especially between mates.

Flame-templed Babbler

(Stachyris speciosa)

IUCN: Endangered

Length: 6–6½ in. (15–16.5 cm) (estimated)

Weight: Unknown

Clutch size: Unknown

Incubation: Unknown

Diet: Unknown

Habitat: Forest and forest edges up to 3,200 ft. (975 m) elevation

Range: Negros Island in the Philippines

THE PHILIPPINES are made up of thousands of islands. Many of them are quite mountainous, and most of them were at one time thickly forested.

For many years, more new birds were discovered in these forests than anywhere else on

earth. Ornithologists long suspected more were yet to be discovered, but so much of the Philippine forests have been cut for lumber and cleared for agriculture that no one can be sure how many unknown species disappeared before anyone even knew they existed. Certainly many known species have dwindled. Ornithologists believe that birds unique to single islands are particularly vulnerable to habitat loss. The flame-templed babbler is one of them.

Colorful details

Overall, the flame-templed babbler is a dull golden or straw color. However, it also has a gray-green back that is finely streaked in dull white. The wing, rump, and tail are a dull brownish green, and the breast and belly are olive. The chin, cheek, eye ring, lore, and forehead are yellow, as is the spotted throat. The crown and back of the head are

Babblers are a diverse group of small songbirds. This bird, a relative of Hinde's pied babbler, is the arrow-marked babbler (*Turdoides jardineii*).

black, and the nape is black as well, giving the bird a collared appearance. There is a bright orange tuft over the eye. The beak is light orange.

Island deforestation

The flame-templed babbler inhabits the small tracts of forest remaining on Negros Island. The Philippines' fourth largest island, Negros covers 5,278 square miles (13,670 square kilometers) and rises to a little more than 8,070 feet (2,460 meters) at Mount Canlaon, a dormant volcano. Negros was originally heavily forested, but it has been drastically affected by tree cutting. The coastal plains were cleared for sugarcane plantations and rice paddies. The montane forests were cut mostly for their valuable tropical woods. People also cut the forest for firewood to cook their food and for construction. In 1940, approximately 1.25 million people lived on Negros. The human population topped 2 million people four decades later. Such a large number of people causes changes in natural landscapes and plant communities. Negros has very little primary forest left, and what does survive is in isolated patches in the mountainous interior.

Conservation needed

Without some restraint in the destructive cutting or foresight to preserve adequate timber stands for forest wildlife, the flame-templed babbler, as well as various other creatures, could be lost.

Hinde's Pied Babbler
(Turdoides hindei)

IUCN: Endangered

Length: 7½–8½ in. (19–22 cm)
Weight: Unknown
Clutch size: Unknown
Incubation: Unknown
Diet: Unknown
Habitat: Sources vary; generally, dense scrub on steep slopes and open woodland
Range: Kenya

INDIVIDUAL HINDE'S PIED babblers exhibit much variation in plumage. This has prompted some speculation that they are either hybrids of the northern pied babbler (*Turdoides hypoleucos*) and the arrow-marked babbler (*T. jardineii*), or that the species arose from such hybrids. These theories currently do not have wide acceptance.

In general, the Hinde's pied babbler is dark brown overall—in fact, it is so dark that it almost seems black. Only the flank, rump, and undertail are lighter, and these are a tawny hue. The breast feathers are tipped with white. The back, wing, tail, crown, neck, and cheek have a peculiar scaled appearance.

Unlike so many other species, Hinde's pied babbler has readily accepted an exotic plant, the lan-

NEGROS BABBLER
Philippines

FLAME-TEMPLED BABBLER
Philippines

HINDE'S PIED BABBLER
Africa

WHITE-BREASTED BABBLER
Indonesia

tana, as its favored habitat. This plant typically grows on steep slopes. Whether the babbler accepts lantana in order to remain on the slopes or remains on the slopes in order to use the lantana is not clear. However, where native plant communities have been cleared from rocky hillsides, the Hinde's pied babbler has disappeared. The bird also readily uses shrubs that grow after forest clearing. In drier woodlands it stays close to riparian, or waterside, thickets.

Typical babbler

In many behavioral respects, the Hinde's pied babbler is a typical babbler. Small flocks of less than a dozen birds, usually six to eight individuals, often occur together and stay within their small territories. These flocks may remain more or less intact even during the breeding season. Individual babblers within the flock have been observed preening each other regularly.

Some confusion lingers about the status of Hinde's pied babbler. A small bird inclined to sit quietly for long periods in thick brush, it may seem rare simply because it is difficult to find rather than because its numbers are declining. Still, farming in Kenya (mostly for maize production) has depleted the natural habitat significantly. As habitat parcels become smaller and more isolated, sedentary birds such as Hinde's pied babbler may be forced to inbreed, and this can reduce the species' long-term chances for survival.

Steps to protect the Hinde's pied babbler will rely largely on determining its actual range limits, current status, and the causes of its decline. Research is imperative to acquire this information.

Negros Babbler
(Stachyris nigrorum)

IUCN: Endangered

Length: Estimated 6 in. (15 cm)
Weight: Unknown
Clutch size: Unknown
Incubation: Unknown
Diet: Unknown
Habitat: Forests above 3,200 ft. (975 m) elevation
Range: Originally believed unique to Negros Island in the Philippines, but now known to live on Panay Island as well

So little is known of the Negros babbler's natural history that even its status as a species is only suspected. However, the Philippine people have been steadily cutting the Negros forests for decades, and a species cannot withstand habitat loss indefinitely. Originally thought to be unique to Negros Island, the Negros babbler was found on Panay, a large island neighboring Negros to the north. Whether it occurs on other islands is not certain, but its preference for forests at higher elevations limits which islands it could inhabit.

The back, wing, and tail of the Negros babbler are a dull olive that appears almost brown; the underparts are mostly a uniform olive-yellow, as are the breast and belly, although they also have dull brown stripes. The throat and cheek are a dingy white, but the cheek has large black spots that almost merge to form a dark patch.

White-breasted Babbler

(Stachyris grammiceps)

IUCN: Vulnerable

Length: 4½ in. (11 cm)
Weight: Unknown
Clutch size: Unknown
Incubation: Unknown
Diet: Unknown
Habitat: Forests
Range: Western Java

Almost nothing is known of the white-breasted babbler other than that it exists. Even early references described it as rare. The small area where it is known to occur, the forested hill country of western Java, has been heavily cut for lumber and cleared for agriculture. Without definite knowledge of the bird's natural history, very little can be said about it with certainty, and recommendations cannot be made to protect it. However, ornithologists agree that the species surely must be affected by the loss of its only known habitat.

Appearance

The underparts of the white-breasted babbler are brown, while the throat, middle breast, and belly are white. The side and undertail of the bird are gray, while the nape, neck, and cheek are a slightly darker shade of gray; the crown is an even darker gray with light streaks.

Kevin Cook

Babirusa

(Babyrousa babyrussa)

IUCN: Endangered

IUCN: Vulnerable

Class: Mammalia
Order: Artiodactyla
Family: Suidae
Weight: 175–220 lb. (80–100 kg)
Shoulder height: 25–31 in. (65–80 cm)
Diet: Omnivorous
Gestation period: 150–160 days
Longevity: 15–20 years
Habitat: Rain forest
Range: Indonesia (Sulawesi, Togian, Buru, and Sula Islands)

The babirusa is one of the more unusual members of the wild swine family. It comes from a relatively small area on the islands of Sulawesi, Togian, Buru, and Sula in Indonesia. It is shy and retiring and is found in forested areas. This species is rarely sighted in the wild.

The striking thing about the male babirusa is its lower canine teeth, which continue to grow throughout its entire life. They grow out of each side of the mouth and curl back toward the animal's back in a long arch.

Even more remarkable is the growth of the upper canines. They actually grow out of the top of the babirusa's snout, or muzzle, instead of growing down. They grow up, out, and back in the same fashion as the lower canines. Older male babirusas exhibit four great teeth, or tusks. Using these tusks, the babirusa

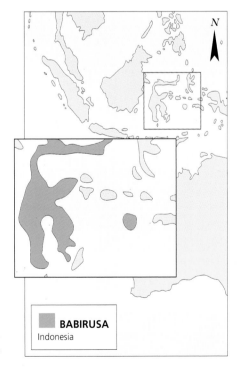

BABIRUSA
Indonesia

does a lot of rubbing and digging. This helps to keep the tips of the tusks worn down.

An interesting legend among the native Sulawesis is that the male babirusa sleeps by hooking his teeth onto a branch so that he suspends himself for the night. This, however, is not true.

The streamlined appearance of the babirusa works well in the heavy tropical bush; it can disappear very quickly into the lush vegetation if surprised.

Unlike the rest of the swine family, the babirusa produces very small litters. Where other swine may have five, six, or even as many as nine offspring, the babirusa routinely produces only one to three (more often two). Babirusas reproduce only once a year. They are not nearly as prolific as many other members of the swine family.

Reproduction in captivity

Babirusas have been held in captivity for some time and do reasonably well. They tend not to reproduce well, however, mainly because managing the new mother is complicated. In most cases, the female needs complete isolation and, unless she has it, may kill her babies or totally ignore them. With complete isolation, she is a good mother.

Like other pigs, babirusas tend to be omnivores. Controversy has arisen about their digestive system, which resembles that of cattle. However, their system is only slightly modified from that of a typical pig. They do not have the four-chambered stomach found in cattle, which means that they are not ruminants.

Population backup

A population of babirusas exists in captivity in Southeast Asia, there is a thriving group in Europe, and a growing population is in North America. However, the European and North American stocks are derived from as few as three animals. Additional wild stock must be brought into captivity to back up wild populations, which are under threat.

Warren D. Thomas

The male babirusa has lower teeth that continue to grow throughout its life, giving it a striking appearance.

Ballota cristata

IUCN: Rare

Family: Labiatae
Stem: Hairy, 6–11 in. (15–28 cm)
Flower: White, about ½ in.
(1 cm) long, the upper lip has a
dense crest of hairs
Rootstock: Woody and
creeping
Habitat: Limestone rocks
in mountains
Range: Antalya, Turkey

BALLOTA CRISTATA IS A medicinal
herb found only in the Antalya
region of Turkey. It grows on
limestone rocks in the mountains

The Antalya region of Turkey is the
preferred habitat of *Ballota cristata*.
The altitude does not deter collectors
from taking the plant.

at an altitude of 3,600 to 5,580
feet (1,100 to 1,700 meters). The
main threat to the species is collection for the medicinal plant
trade. Collection takes place in
spring, and there are concerns
that as well as threatening populations of the species, honey
production is also negatively
affected. Plants are mixed with a
species of origanum, *Origanum
onites*, and are exported as *kekik*.
Collection is undertaken by all
members of the family in the
countryside villages and provides
an important source of income.

Medicinal plant

Ballota cristata is one of 347
Turkish plants collected for medicinal use and is considered to be
one of the top 50 threatened
medicinal plants in that country.
Some actions are needed to conserve and protect medicinal

BALLOTA
CRISTATA
Europe/Asia

plants there. The measures
should include more research to
gain a better understanding of
the trade and its impact on individual species, and cultivation of
threatened species. Ideally local
people would still earn money
from selling the plants without
overharvesting them from the
wild, and protected reserves
would be established for the
threatened species.

Sara Oldfield

Western Barred Bandicoot

(Perameles bougainville)

ESA: Endangered

IUCN: Endangered

Class: Mammalia
Order: Marsupialia
Family: Peramelidae
Weight: 6½–8¾ oz. (180–250 g)
Head-body length: 7½–8¼ in. (19–21 cm)
Diet: Omnivorous
Gestation period: 12½ days
Longevity: 2 to 3 years
Habitat: Dry to semi-arid areas, heaths, and dune vegetation
Range: Two islands off the west coast of Australia

ALTHOUGH ITS name loosely translates as "pig rat," the western barred bandicoot is a marsupial, not a rodent. This species is related to the kangaroo, wallaby, and bettong, which have pouches for carrying their young. The animal is thought to resemble a rat because it has a long, pointed snout, naked ears, and a hairy tail and is about the same size as the common rat. However, its larger hind legs and feet, designed to carry most of its body weight, look much like those of its kangaroo relatives.

The western barred bandicoot, or little marl (an Australian name), has a thickset body with a short neck, a gray back with a subtle bar pattern near the rump, and a white belly and legs. The hind feet each have five toes. The first toe is poorly developed and has no nail. The second and third toes are fused together into a split claw that is used for combing ticks and lice from the fur. The fourth, or main claw, is the largest, and the fifth claw is slightly smaller. The bandicoot's hind legs are more developed than its forelegs, and it runs with many quick changes of direction. It has an elongated snout with 46 to 48 teeth, like the three other long-nosed bandicoots in the genus *Perameles.*

Western barred bandicoots make nests in grassy tussocks or mounds of sticks and leaves. They are solitary, coming out at night in search of food. In this quest, they are aided by a keen sense of smell. Their diet consists of seeds, roots, bulbs, snails, slugs, grubs, caterpillars, earthworms, and occasionally mice.

The gestation period for the western barred bandicoot is uncertain, but its close relative, the long-nosed bandicoot, *P. nasuta*, gives birth in 12½ days—perhaps the shortest gestation period of any mammal. Embryos attach to the uterine wall by means of a placenta, a feature that among marsupials is only found in bandicoots. The young (1 to 5) are tiny at birth, weighing 0.3 gram. With the aid of large claws, it takes them three days to crawl into the pouch, where they suckle on one of eight teats. They stay inside the mother's pouch for a month, until they are able to move around. When they emerge, they quickly return to the pouch at any sign of danger. The pouch of the bandicoot opens between the hind legs and faces towards the rear, which is the opposite of the kangaroo. In three to five months these animals are sexually mature.

Island populations

Because they may dig holes in gardens, bandicoots are considered pests; however, they are probably beneficial because they eat harmful insects. Although Aborigines considered them a delicacy, their decline appears to coincide with the arrival of European settlers. This bandicoot formerly occurred across southern Australia, but today it occurs only in depleted numbers on Bernier and Dorre Islands, off the coast of western Australia. Vegetation that shielded and fed them is mostly gone because of grazing rabbits and land clearing for agriculture. This, combined with the spread of non-native foxes, cats, and rats, has brought the western barred bandicoot to the brink of extinction.

Terry Tompkins

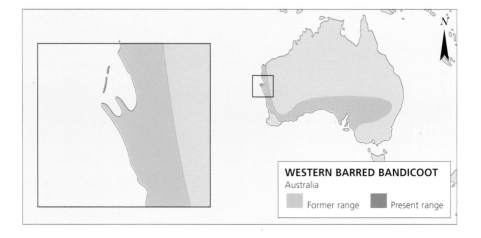

WESTERN BARRED BANDICOOT
Australia

Former range   Present range

Banteng (Tsaine)

(Bos javanicus)

ESA: Endangered

IUCN: Endangered

Class: Mammalia
Order: Artiodactyla
Family: Bovidae
Weight: 1,320–1,870 lb. (600–850 kg)
Shoulder height: 55–70 in. (140–180 cm)
Diet: Grass, leaves, and twigs
Gestation period: 280–295 days
Longevity: 25 years
Habitat: Dense forest to open glades
Range: Southeast Asia

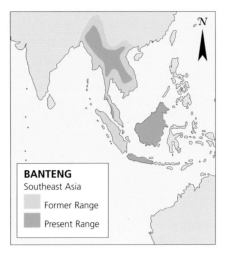

BANTENG
Southeast Asia

Former Range

Present Range

THE BANTENG IS ONE of the larger members of the wild cattle family, and it has a broad geographical range, encompassing Myanmar (formerly Burma), Thailand, Laos, Cambodia, Vietnam, western Malaysia, Borneo, and the Indonesian islands of Java and Bali.

The male banteng becomes very dark or brownish purple with white markings on the rump and belly. The female is a fawn brown. Both sexes have horns.

Banteng range in meadows and retreat to dense forest. They are found in small herds within the confines of the forest and occasionally can be seen running with other wild cattle and even deer. In Cambodia, banteng have also been seen in the company of kouprey (*Bos sauveli*). Banteng produce one calf each year.

The primary threat to the banteng is its shrinking habitat. Its normal forest habitat is being

Part of the banteng's range was assaulted by the lengthy Vietnam war, which took a heavy toll on the wildlife in Southeast Asia.

cut down and food sources destroyed, so it wanders out into the countryside to forage, where it comes into contact with humans. Poaching the horns for profit is the result.

Hybridization is another problem. The banteng will breed with domestic cattle, and in Indonesia there is a domesticated form of banteng that further reduces the wild gene pool.

There are some good stocks of banteng in captivity. However, there is much uncertainty whether these are purebred wild bantengs. It appears that a number of these animals were simply domesticated stock that were hybridized with domestic cattle.

Latest estimates by the IUCN Asian Wild Cattle Specialist Group suggest that the world population of banteng is possibly less than 5,000. Numbers in Thailand since 1975 have decreased by 80 percent, and this is probably the case over much of the banteng's range. Those remaining are in small fragmented populations, with no chance for outbreeding. The future of wild banteng is definitely vulnerable, and the lack of a sound captive population only increases its uncertain future.

Warren D. Thomas

Because many banteng in captivity are thought to be a mix of banteng and domestic cattle, the captive population offers little security against extinction.

BARBS

Class: Actinopterygii

Order: Cypriniformes

Family: Cyprinidae

Barbs are part of the large family Cyprinidae. Although most of these fish are small minnows that rarely exceed 5–6 inches (13–15 centimeters), this group also includes the giant mahseer (*Barbus tor*), which may exceed 5 feet (1.5 meters) in length and can weigh over 100 pounds (45 kilograms). This so-called minnow, a sport fish in India, is usually found in the slow, meandering rivers of southern India, but it migrates to the clear mountain streams of the Himalayas to spawn.

Barbs are quite important ecologically because they are often found in great numbers, serving as an important food item for other fishes, reptiles, birds, and mammals. Unfortunately, they are often victims of non-native fish introduced into their waters by people. Many barbs are presently threatened due to loss of habitat, introduction of non-native fish, and capture for the aquarium trade.

Like most Cyprinidae, barbs are often found in schools and generally prefer clear water. The females scatter their eggs over vegetation and, in most species, a special sticky outer layer of the eggs allows them to attach to aquatic plants. Males fertilize the eggs by spreading their sperm (milt) over the eggs.

Most barbs have two fleshy barbels (feelers) on each side of the mouth, but some have only one or none at all. Because of their small size, bright colors, and prolific reproduction in captivity, the barbs have become favorites of aquarium enthusiasts. Males are often brilliantly colored during spawning and exhibit involved courting behavior, adding to their desirability.

Barbs have no teeth in the mouth, but in the back of the throat are comb-like teeth, called pharyngeal teeth.

Black Ruby Barb

(Puntius nigrofasciatus)

IUCN: Lower risk

Length: 2½ in. (6 cm)
Reproduction: Egg layer
Habitat: Clear, fast-flowing streams of moderate size
Range: Sri Lanka

THE COLORFUL and active black ruby barb is found in three large river systems in southwest Sri Lanka: Gin Ganga, Kalu Ganga, and Kelani Ganga. In recent decades, much of the native range of this barb has been drastically altered due to deforestation. This small fish is one of many native species of Sri Lanka to suffer, although it has now been classified by IUCN–The World Conservation Union as lower risk.

In areas that have been spared from deforestation, fishing for the black ruby barb to support the aquarium trade has further reduced its numbers and increased the probability of its extinction. Human colonization, resulting in biological and chemical polluting of streams, also has had a negative impact. The last stronghold of the black ruby barb is in, and adjacent to, the Kenneliya Forest Reserve in the basin of Gin Ganga in Sri Lanka.

The black ruby barb gets its name from the distinct dark purple-red color of the head area of courting males, which is complemented by its black body and fins. As in most members of the

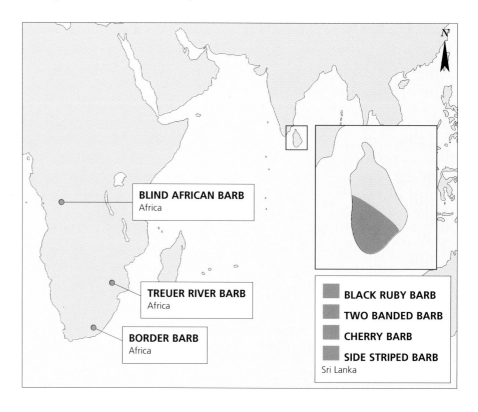

BLIND AFRICAN BARB
Africa

TREUER RIVER BARB
Africa

BORDER BARB
Africa

BLACK RUBY BARB
TWO BANDED BARB
CHERRY BARB
SIDE STRIPED BARB
Sri Lanka

minnow family (Cyprinidae), there is a contrast between the sexes, particularly in times of spawning. This difference in appearance between males and females, called sexual dimorphism, is quite common in many fishes. The males show more coloration and have larger fins. The females have more of a dark gray color on the body and are much lighter on the belly. In addition, the females lack the striking purple-red color on the head. Immature fish have three distinct dark vertical bands on the side of the body and no coloration on the head at all. In general, this barb has a thin body, relatively large fins, and a small, sharply pointed head.

The black ruby barb can be found either in groups or alone in most parts of streams and creeks during all times of the day. Most of its energy is spent foraging on various forms of minute aquatic organisms, while avoiding natural predators such as larger fish, birds, and water snakes.

These rare minnows are able to reproduce year-round, but during the annual monsoon (rainy) season, most quiet, clear, vegetated backwaters required for mating become turbulent and muddy. During these high-flow events, the black ruby barb is believed to seek shelter in the stream bottoms as it waits for calmer conditions to return.

Interaction between males before the courtship ritual is quite interesting. An encounter between two or more males stimulates an increase in coloration. Previously dull colors become strikingly vibrant, and the brilliant purple-red head takes on an iridescent character. The competing males swim in tight circles with occasional nips at the fins of their rivals until one has established dominance. Once the pecking order is established, they become quite calm, and the successful male begins to court his potential mate.

Courtship display

Attired in his splendid courtship colors, the male black ruby barb constantly circles the female, making repeated displays. Eventually the female is driven to an area with aquatic plants, where eggs and sperm are released simultaneously above the vegetation. After mating, the pair separate for a brief time. Then the male again drives the female toward the plants, where a second group of eggs are dropped over the aquatic plants.

This behavior is repeated several times, for a period of up to two hours, or until the female has exhausted her supply of eggs. The bright colors of the male then fade and become rather dull, and normal activities associated with feeding are resumed. The females will be ready to spawn again in about two weeks.

Barbs are actually minnows that prefer to swim in schools. They are popular aquarium fish, and this has contributed to the declining numbers of many species within the family of Cyprinidae.

On average, development of the eggs is accomplished in about 30 hours, but this may vary with water temperature. The maturing larvae remain attached to the stems or leaves of the plants for about three days. After this time they begin to swim freely and start to feed on the smallest of aquatic organisms.

Ironically, it is the elaborate mating ritual that has contributed to the sharp decline of the black ruby barb. In the few areas of southern Sri Lanka that have been spared the devastation of deforestation, natives capture the small minnows and export them. The brilliant coloration and involved courting behavior make this fish a prize for aquarium enthusiasts.

Although captive breeding is readily accomplished and could help sustain the species, it would be a tragedy if, in the future, these small fish were no longer found in their native habitat of southern Sri Lanka.

Blind African Barb

(Caecobarbus geertsi)

IUCN: Vulnerable

Length: 2¾ in. (7 cm)
Reproduction: Egg layer
Longevity: 20–30 years
Habitat: Fresh water
Range: Cave at Thysville, Democratic Republic of Congo

THE VERY DISTINCT blind African barb is found naturally in only one cave in central Africa. Thus, its native range is extremely limited. It occurs in small numbers, making it rare enough to be considered vulnerable by international conservation groups. A few of these fish are found in public aquaria, so there is a measure of protection if something should happen to threaten their survival in the cave at Thysville. They are considered a valuable resource, and extensive measures have been taken to ensure their survival. This is important because any change in their environment could signal disaster.

Adding to potential problems associated with their extremely limited native range, their uniqueness has made them vulnerable to illegal capture for aquarium hobbyists. Although they are indeed protected, as is the case in many underdeveloped countries, a small bribe will often be enough to bend the rules. Because of this, many of the blind African barbs have been removed from the cave in which they are found.

There is no light in this underground home, so this small minnow lacks two things that nearly all other barbs possess: eyes and coloration on the body. The blind African barb is a very pale pink species with rather large fins and two prominent feelers (barbels), one on each side of the mouth. It uses these barbels to help it find food. Constantly on the move, the blind African barb must seek and recognize its prey. Most of the time it finds some small aquatic organisms called zooplankton. Given the chance, however, it will consume small fish as well. It has even been observed to engage in cannibalism.

Sightlessness

Lack of eyes is not uncommon in nature. Many organisms that have evolved in an underground environment have either not developed eyes or have lost them over many years of gradual change. Long ago the ancestors of these small barbs looked more like typical minnows. Over many generations, the eyes slowly degenerated until they disappeared entirely. Examples similar to this can be found in many other groups of fish.

The blind African barb requires water that is between 70 and 85 degrees Fahrenheit (21 and 29 degrees Centigrade). It is capable of reproducing throughout the year at intervals of 30 days. Since it is unable to see, there is no dramatic color change in the males at spawning time, as is the case with nearly all other barbs. Eggs are ready to hatch within a few days of being laid, and the fry often become a food source for the parents.

The cave at Thysville is a relatively large natural cave known for its beauty. It is maintained as a national park of sorts, although not many visitors enjoy its unique wonders. With some luck, these interesting and rare little blind fish will remain an important part of this exceptional natural environment.

Border Barb

(Barbus trevelyani)

IUCN: Critically endangered

Length: 4 in. (10 cm)
Reproduction: Egg layer
Habitat: Pools and backwater of clear rivers and streams
Range: Amatola Mountains, southeastern Africa

NAMED FOR THE striking borders that highlight the outer edges of its fins, the border barb (*Barbus trevelyani*) is the victim of a continually shrinking habitat. It is found only in the Amatola Mountains of the eastern Cape of South Africa. Recent agricultural development in the region has placed strong demand on the aquatic resources of the general region. Because of uneven rainfall and the steep mountain valleys, farmers are forced to depend on stream and river diversions to irrigate their crops, thereby causing some tributaries to become completely dry at certain times of the year. Streams are regulated by dams and weirs, and often bulldozers are used to channelize the streams to facilitate irrigation. This has severe negative impacts on the fish found in these areas.

New predators

A second major problem for the border barb is the introduction of non-native fish into its waters. Much of its limited range is in the headwaters and higher elevations of the Amatola Mountains. These streams are capable of supporting rainbow trout (*Oncorhynchus mykiss*), which find the border barbs easy prey. Trout have been stocked throughout the world to provide recreation and, until recently, little attention was paid to the secondary effects of placing trout in waters where they did not occur naturally. In many cases, smaller fish like the border barb disappear altogether from rivers and streams where they had lived for thousands of years.

Predators such as non-native fish may also become a problem as a result of unintentional introduction. For example, the sharptooth catfish (*Clarias gariepinus*) was recently brought to South Africa to provide food. Although intended to be contained in aquaculture facilities, a few were able to find their way into some streams in the home range of the border barb. Much like trout, these catfish are very opportunistic feeders and will feast upon small fish when they are available. The end result is disaster for the border barb, a small victim that is already declining due to loss of habitat.

A slender fish

The border barb is a slender and lean minnow that has dark bands on the outer edges of its fins. This edging is more pronounced in males, allowing the sexes to be easily distinguishable. The fish prefers backwaters and slow-moving pools in the streams and rivers of the Amatola Mountains.

Like many fish in South Africa, the border barb is critically endangered and is very vulnerable to extinction. Because of the global trend toward human overpopulation, it is unlikely that the intense demand on water resources will be eased in the near future. As demand for water increases, the prospect for improving the status of the border barb, as well as other endangered fish, remains gloomy.

Cherry Barb
(Puntius titteya)

IUCN: Lower risk

Length: 2 in. (5 cm)
Reproduction: Egg layer
Habitat: Small streams and creeks
Range: Southern Sri Lanka

THE CHERRY BARB is a favorite of aquarium keepers. It is widely available at tropical fish and pet stores, but in its native home in Sri Lanka it is rapidly disappearing. The combined threat of deforestation and overharvest place this colorful barb in a precarious position in the wild. Much of southern Sri Lanka is being cleared for agricultural use. What was once a dense tropical forest has been either clear-cut, bulldozed, or burned to make way for cattle or crops. The result is often tragic for wild inhabitants of these areas. The cherry barb is just one of many victims of this practice. To add insult to injury, in the few reserves that have been spared deforestation, the cherry barb is actively pursued by local fishers. Once captured, it is exported to developed countries, where the small barb is prized as an aquarium fish.

Striking coloration

As the name suggests, this barb is noted for its red coloration. Coloration, however, depends on the mood and spawning condition of the individual. It varies from deep cherry red to a dull light brown, with all shades in between. Males are always a few shades brighter than females, especially when reproductively active. Their fins take on deep red shades. They also have a black stripe that crosses the length of the body, stopping just before the tail fin. The stripe passes through the eye, giving an unusual accent to the head.

Prior to spawning, the males become particularly active as they swim in tight, furious circles. During this period, the color of the male intensifies to a vibrant ox-blood hue. It seems to glow like a light. And although some of the richness fades just after the males spawn, the intensified color often lasts for several hours. Curiously, the dark lateral band often disappears at this time as well.

Detailed feeding studies of the cherry barb in Sri Lanka have revealed that this tiny barb feeds on a wide variety of organisms, including some plant material. Small aquatic insects are the favored food item, and fish eggs are often an additional component. Because this fish shares its habitat with another barb, the two spotted barb (*Puntius bimaculatus*), both have adjusted their feeding habits so as not to overlap. This is not uncommon when similar fish occupy the same habitat. By slightly adjusting the type of food they consume, competition between the two species is reduced. Both are able to benefit from such an arrangement.

Aquarium fish

As previously discussed, the appeal of the cherry barb to fish hobbyists has contributed to its decline in the wild. It has the reputation of being a very peaceful inhabitant of a mixed aquarium and ranks at the top of the list of barbs that have become popular in recent years.

It also brings a distinct element of beauty to a fish tank. Its sense of community probably is a result of its innate tendency to form groups, or schools, in the wild. Because this barb will reproduce quite easily in captivity, there is little need to capture live wild fish from the streams and creeks of southern Sri Lanka. However, in poorer, less developed areas, if a profit can be gained by trapping these popular little minnows, it will no doubt continue.

Side Striped Barb

(Puntius pleurotaenia)

IUCN: Lower risk

Length: 4⅓ in. (11 cm)
Reproduction: Egg layer
Longevity: 20–30 years
Habitat: Clear streams and creeks
Range: Southern Sri Lanka

THE RELATIVELY LARGE side striped barb has a small natural range in the southern part of Sri Lanka. It is found in three large river systems which include Gin Ganga, Kalu Ganga, and Kelani Ganga. Perhaps the greatest threat to the side striped barb, however, is the dramatic loss of habitat from deforestation. This barb is not alone in its plight. Many species of plants and animals have become threatened due to this practice of clearing tropical forests. Encroachment by civilization into this once pristine area of Sri Lanka has also produced a certain amount of pollution of the streams this small fish calls home.

Another significant threat comes from consumption of the side striped barb by the indigenous peoples of Sri Lanka. The combination of overharvest and loss of habitat has put this fish in a precarious situation—although it is now considered to be at lower risk of extinction—and conservation organizations have taken measures to protect it from future decline.

The side striped barb receives its name from the prominent dark band that dominates the side of its body. It is one of the largest fish in the genus *Puntius*, which makes it a desirable fish for consumption. While other barbs found in the same streams as the side striped barb are frequently caught and exported for aquarists, this robust minnow is rarely allowed to escape the dining table.

The side striped barb is found to inhabit mountain streams and creeks with very clear water. It appears to prefer quiet backwaters and deep, slow-moving pools where the water is relatively calm. This barb is rarely observed swimming against a strong current. It is more likely to be seen in a mixed school with another minnow (*Rasbora daniconius*), and often it is difficult to distinguish between the two. The side striped barb would rather hide in a shaded corner of the stream and refrain from basking in sunlit waters. An active swimmer, it is seldom taken in a handheld net. People are able to capture this elusive minnow by throwing a castnet over a pool believed to be holding them.

Colorful males

Males become more active and colorful while spawning, as is the case with most members of the minnow family. The generally good-natured male becomes very aggressive and will chase and nip competing males in the territory it considers its own. Once a male has established his area, any female that enters this domain will be actively pursued. If the female is ready to spawn, she will often be directed toward the nearest aquatic plant, but dense mats of floating algae are preferred. The breeding pair release eggs and sperm simultaneously, and the eggs adhere to the submerged vegetation. The pair will often rest for a moment, then repeat the entire process several times until all of the female's eggs are released.

It takes only one or two days for the tiny fry to emerge, but the larval fish (newly hatched, with yolk-sac) remain stuck to the aquatic plants for three more days. The fry then leave the security of the plants and begin their search for food.

Treur River Barb

(Barbus treurensis)

IUCN: Lower risk

Length: 3¾in. (9.5 cm)
Reproduction: Egg layer
Longevity: 20–30 years
Habitat: Pools and backwaters of small rivers and streams
Range: Blyde River, South Africa

THE TREUR RIVER BARB was first discovered in 1958 in the South African river whose name it bears. The Treur River is a tributary of the Blyde River, located in South Africa in a region known as the Transvaal. The barb is now extinct from the Treur River, but it can be found in a three-mile section of the Blyde River above a 60-foot (18-meter) waterfall.

The stocking of two non-native game fish, smallmouth bass (*Micropterus dolomieu*) and rainbow trout (*Oncorhynchus mykiss*), invariably results in local extinction of this small barb. This is one of many instances where the introduction of a non-native sport fish has been a disaster for the local fauna. The impact, in this particular situation, is compounded by the extremely small natural range of the Treur River barb. With a few exceptions, most of the rivers that this fish inhabits have been proclaimed trout areas by the Republic of South Africa. The planting and harvesting of pine trees (also not native to South Africa) in the Transvaal is another factor that poses a potential threat to the long-term survival of this species. The trees themselves are not harmful to the fish, but before these decorative trees are planted, vast areas of existing vegetation are cut and removed. This logging activity causes soil erosion and sedimentation in streams, decreasing the quality of habitat for the Treur River barb.

Fortunately, there is a short reach of the Blyde River, about three miles (5 kilometers), where the Treur River barb is considered to be stable. After winding through a large section of private land (owned by the Mousi Timber Company), the Blyde River cascades over a 60-foot (18-meter) waterfall. Below this fall, trout are abundant and the tiny barb cannot be found. No trout or bass have been stocked above this waterfall and, to protect the Treur River barb, no future stocking is intended. Although this is a very restricted distribution, the species is abundant in this limited area. This short section of the Blyde River was also designated a Natural Heritage Site in 1985. Instituted as a means to conserve endangered or vulnerable fish and wildlife on private lands in South Africa, the Natural Heritage Site concept has proven to be of great benefit to this little barb.

Although the Treur River barb has been totally eliminated from the area where it was discovered, it is abundant and thriving within the Natural Heritage Site. It is now considered to be at lower risk of endangerment. To further stabilize the situation, a number of fish have been transplanted to a secure habitat in one of the nature reserves of the Transvaal Nature Conservation Division on the Transvaal escarpment.

The Treur River barb is a small minnow about 4 inches (10 centimeters) in length. As the name suggests, it has two barbels on each side of the mouth. Males and females can be distinguished by their different coloration, particularly when reproducing. The fins of the male become dark, and bumps (tubercles) appear on and near the head.

Quiet pools

The Treur River barb prefers the quiet backwaters and calmer pools in the Blyde River drainage, and is often found in aggregations sheltered by aquatic plants. It requires submerged vegetation for protection and feeding, as well as for a place for females to deposit eggs. It prefers warmer water, between 70 and 80 degrees Fahrenheit (21 to 26 Centigrade), but will tolerate colder temperatures. Eggs hatch quickly, within 2 to 3 days, and the fry often hide in dense mats of floating algae or moss.

Two Banded Barb

(Puntius cumingii)

IUCN: Lower risk

Length: 2 in. (5 cm)
Reproduction: Egg layer
Longevity: 20–30 years
Habitat: Streams and creeks
Range: Southwest Sri Lanka

THE TWO BANDED BARB is native to southwestern Sri Lanka. Although it is currently quite rare in its natural environment, it is popular as an aquarium fish, both in and outside of Sri Lanka. The main threat to this small colorful barb comes from the ongoing practice of deforestation of much of its native range. Furthermore, encroachment by civilization both for colonization and agriculture has caused a large number of streams and creeks in southern Sri Lanka to become degraded and polluted.

Illegal capture

Loss of habitat is a significant problem that is further compounded by the uncontrolled catching of this tiny minnow by fish hobbyists and those who sell live fish for the aquarium trade. It is a tragic course of events, because when fish are exported from Sri Lanka for this purpose, many die before reaching their destinations. There are some areas of Sri Lanka that have been set aside as nature reserves, such as the Kenneliya Forest Reserve, but illegal capture of these minnows still occurs within the boundaries of the reserve.

As the name suggests, the two banded barb has two prominent dark bands around the body: one just in front of the tail and one near the center of the fish. This small but robust barb typically shows slightly different intensity of coloration between males and females. This difference becomes quite apparent when the fish become reproductively active. Males display a dramatically heightened intensity of color. There is also a slight difference between the sexes in body shape, as the males are slightly rounded. The fins of the two banded barb

are bright orange or yellow, which is more pronounced in spawning males. There is some indication that two varieties of the two banded barb exist in different areas of Sri Lanka. Not enough is known about the extent of the differences, however, to conclude whether these are two subspecies or just subtle variations of one species.

This attractive minnow is often found in large groups or schools, and tends to prefer quiet backwaters. Occasionally the two banded barb will find its way to a still pool near the center of the stream, but most of its time is spent very close to the edges, where the shelter of aquatic vegetation is found. It must be on the alert for such natural predators as water snakes, kingfishers, and a new enemy: humans.

Like most barbs that reside in a tropical environment, the two banded barb is capable of spawning throughout the year. It requires specific temperatures and quality of water to stimulate spawning, and there is some indication that there may be a seasonal nature to its reproduc-

tion, because of the annual pattern of monsoon rains. Releasing the eggs at a time that would favor their chances for survival is a typical reproductive strategy of many kinds of fish.

Courtship is a complex and consuming behavior for the two banded barb. Competition between males for the right to spawn is a never-ending process. By breeding with only the strongest males, the female ensures that her offspring will have a better chance at survival. Females lay eggs near or above submerged plants, where the eggs attach themselves to the vegetation with a special adhesive outer layer. The small hatchlings usually stay close to the plant cover for some time after hatching.

The beauty of the two banded barb is the reason that has promoted its capture by aquarists. The ease with which it exists in captivity may be a beneficial factor, if it makes it possible to return this fish to the wild. The trick will be to keep its native rivers and streams in a natural and healthy state.

Donald S. Proebstel

Barbs have no teeth, but in the back of the throat they do have comblike protrusions called pharyngeal teeth.

Dalmatian Barbelgudgeon

(Aulopyge hugeli)

IUCN: Vulnerable

Class: Actinopterygii
Order: Cypriniformes
Family: Cyprinidae
Length: 8 in. (20 cm)
Reproduction: Egg layer
Longevity: 20–30 years
Habitat: Rivers and lakes
Range: Bosnia-Herzegovina, Croatia

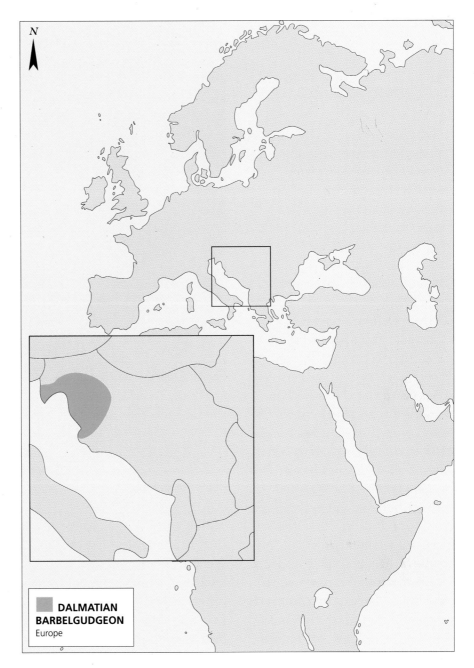

DALMATIAN BARBELGUDGEON
Europe

THE DALMATIAN barbelgudgeon belongs to the diverse family of fish called Cyprinidae, which includes carp, minnows, shiners, daces, barbs, chubs, and similar groups. Worldwide, there are over 1,500 species of Cyprinidae, and many are found in Europe.

Loss of habitat

Threats to the Dalmatian barbelgudgeon include pollution, fluctuating water levels that appear to harm the young of this species, and loss of habitat from the construction of dams and reservoirs. The Zrmanja River in Croatia has been particularly hard hit by human development activity. This fish prefers to inhabit rivers but has been forced to occupy reservoirs as the number of dams on its native rivers increases. Research indicates that this fish is locally abundant, but its habitat is rapidly being depleted. Cyprinids are inherently tough, but the future for the Dalmatian barbelgudgeon looks bleak. Eastern European countries are determined to increase their standard of living through the development of energy supplies such as hydroelectric power, so it is unlikely that priority will be given to the survival of a rare fish species.

Unknown ecology

Few details about this fish's life are known. All cyprinids, including this fish, have a peculiar organ called the Weberian apparatus. This curious internal body part is comprised of a series of bones that connect the fish's gas bladder to its inner ear. It is probably responsible for this fish's keen sense of hearing. In addition to its job in regulating buoyancy, the gas bladder acts as an amplifier of sound, like a drum, for the Weberian apparatus. These amplified sounds are then carried to the ear.

One particularly curious behavioral habit of the Dalmatian barbelgudgeon is its annual winter migration to underground streams. The purpose of this migration is unknown.

William E. Manci

Toucan Barbet
(Semnornis ramphastinus)

IUCN: Lower risk

Class: Aves
Order: Piciformes
Family: Capitonidae
Length: 8 in. (20 cm)
Weight: Unknown
Clutch size: Unknown
Incubation: Unknown
Diet: Unknown
Habitat: Wet tropical forests, particularly forest edges
Range: Western Andes in Colombia, southward into Ecuador

BARBETS QUALIFY among the most colorful of all birds. Bright patches of red or blue often adorn their faces and heads. The toucan barbet is black around the base of the beak and eyes, on the crown, and down the neck to form an incomplete collar. The cheeks, chin, throat, and neck are a neutral gray; the rump is yellow, contrasting sharply with the straw-brown back. The breast and belly are red or reddish, while the flanks and lower belly are yellow-green. The wings and tail are green to gray-green. The beak is thick and yellowish with a black ring at the tip. These birds are characterized by large heads, stout beaks, short legs, and feet with two toes pointing forward and two backward. Their wings are short and rounded.

The toucan barbet flies with rapid wing beats, but its flight is weak, covering only short distances. It often sits quietly and nearly motionless for long periods in trees. At other times, it

The beautiful appearance of the toucan barbet has led to it being prized as a unique and unusual pet. Unfortunately, many birds are taken from the wild to meet the demand for this exotic species.

moves freely with either mixed flocks containing many forest species or in small groups of its own kind. Males in breeding condition have been found from February into May, and juvenile birds have been seen in May. This suggests that the species begins breeding in late February or March. As do many of its kin, the toucan barbet nests in tree cavities, which makes it dependent upon forests.

Caged bird trade
Tropical forests in the toucan's range are being cut by people, but enough remains so that habitat loss does not account for the species' decline. The toucan barbet owes its population loss to its great beauty. Many people prize the toucan barbet for its brilliant coloration, and, unfortunately, it is easily trapped to accommodate this demand. Since the demand remains stable while the supply dwindles, its price goes up. This only adds incentive to those who deal with caged birds illegally. National parks and forest reserves protect habitat for toucan barbets, and it is now at lower risk, but for future security, the birds must be guarded against poaching.

Kevin Cook

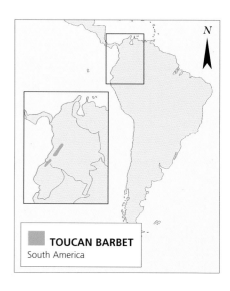

TOUCAN BARBET
South America

BATS

Class: Mammalia

Order: Chiroptera

To most people the mention of bats conjures up images from folklore and scary stories. The sight of a flying bat often makes people squeamish. Yet such fears are largely based on ignorance. Here are some facts that contradict these fears:

Bats are not blind, but in fact can see very well, and some species see better than others. When they cannot see prey, such as in the dark, bats use a radar system known as echolocation.

The bat emits sound waves, which bounce off its prey, then the bat hears an echo, which locates the insect. The bat needs good hearing for this procedure.

With a few exceptions, bats rarely contract and spread diseases like rabies—much less often than animals such as skunks, raccoons, dogs, and cats. Bats, like domestic pets, groom themselves quite frequently.

Bats are not flying rodents, but they are mammals that have a role to play in the balance of nature. Like birds, they consume many insects and help to control several pests that spread disease and damage crops. A single brown bat has been estimated to catch and eat over 600 flying insects in an hour. A colony of 20 million bats can eat over 500,000 pounds (227,000 kilograms) of insects in one night. Bats eat fruits and seeds and help to spread new vegetation by dispersing undigested seeds. Many cultivated plants and trees such as banana, avocado, fig, and peach depend on bats to help with pollination.

Despite the importance of bats to the global ecology, about 40 percent of these creatures are considered endangered, and many species may be extinct. There are many families of bats, but those listed here are all from the family Vespertilionidae.

Gray Bat

(Myotis grisescens)

| **ESA:** Endangered |
| **IUCN:** Endangered |

Weight: ¼–½ oz. (7–16 g)

Length: 1½–4 in. (3.5–10 cm), excluding tail

Diet: Flying insects

Gestation period: 60 days, after delayed fertilization

Longevity: 4–8 years

Habitat: Limestone caves near water

Range: Southeastern United States

THE GRAY BAT IS the largest member of its genus in the eastern United States. After molting in July or August, the gray bat's fur is dark gray, but this usually fades to a chestnut brown or russet shading soon afterward. Unlike other bats, the dorsal fur of the gray bat is uniform in color. The fur of eastern bats shows different colors. The gray bat also differs from other bats in the genus *Myotis* because its wing membrane connects to the foot at the ankle rather than at the base of the first toe.

The gray bat occupies a limited range in the southeastern United States, preferring to live in limestone caves near running water. As with most bats, its choices for roosting are strict, and only about 5 percent of caves meet this species' requirements. This range includes the states of Alabama, Arkansas, Kentucky, Missouri, and Tennessee. A few occur in northwestern Florida, Georgia, the southernmost part of Indiana, Illinois, the northwestern portion of Oklahoma,

Gray bats are dark gray immediately after molting, but their fur quickly changes to chestnut brown or russet.

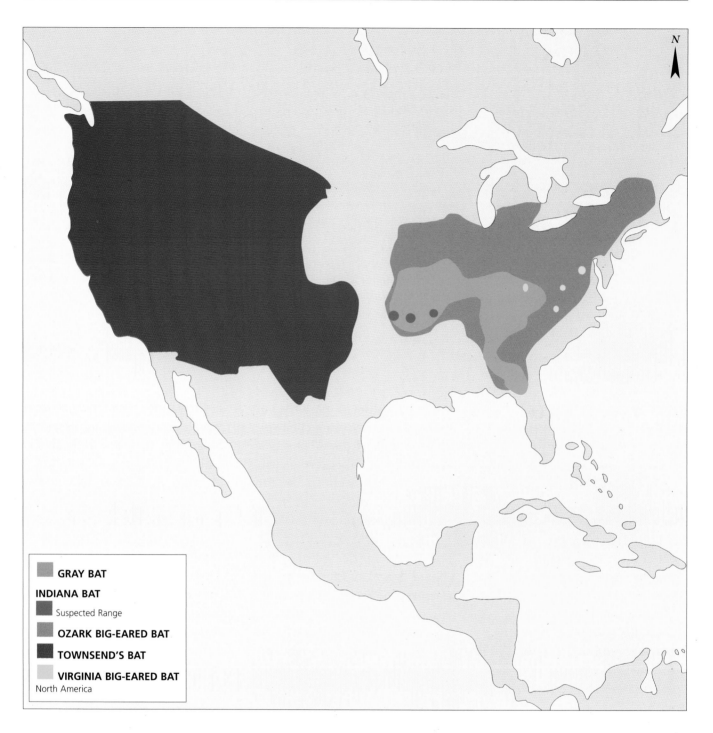

GRAY BAT

INDIANA BAT

Suspected Range

OZARK BIG-EARED BAT

TOWNSEND'S BAT

VIRGINIA BIG-EARED BAT

North America

southeastern Kansas, Mississippi, and the western sections of Virginia and North Carolina. The distribution has always been patchy, but this bat is now becoming increasingly isolated.

In 1970 the population of gray bats was about 2.25 million; this number decreased in the early 1990s to 1.5 million. It is believed that approximately 95 percent of gray bats today hibernate in only

nine caves each winter. Undisturbed summer colonies found in Tennessee and Alabama held between 5,000 and 250,000 bats each. However, most colonies are found to have between 10,000 to 50,000 individuals.

Gray bats, like many bird species, migrate each year. Sometimes they travel as little as 10 miles (16 kilometers) or as far as 150 miles (240 kilometers).

When they arrive at their hibernating caves after fall migration, they will mate and females will then enter hibernation. After mating, males remain active for several weeks, replenishing lost stores of fat. This occurs between late September and early October each year. In late March or early April, adult females emerge. They are then followed by juveniles and adult males to begin migration. From mid-April to mid-May, the females return to summer quarters to bear their young. Body fat may be low after hibernation, and if food supplies are also limited, this can be a time of high mortality.

Reproduction

The female gray bat gives birth to a single offspring in late May or early June. The females establish a nursery in the warmest single cave. Males and nonreproductive females gather in smaller groups in caves around the maternity cave. Nursing reaches its peak when the young are 20 to 30 days old, when they are fed continuously at night. The young bats fly after 20 to 25 days.

The bat feeds on insects at sundown during the peak of insect activity. Feeding may take five to seven hours or may last all night. A single female may control a feeding territory that is occupied by 15 or more bats.

The gray bat appears to be dependent upon aquatic insects such as mosquitoes and mayflies, although it eats other insects. A study at an eastern Tennessee reservoir showed a connection between a high mayfly population and high numbers of foraging bats. Toxic wastes decimate mayfly populations. Gray bats are also dependent upon forestation near waterways. Where the forest is removed, there is a drop in bat population. This may be due to a decrease in food and an increase in predation by owls.

Other forms of human disturbances have contributed to the decline of gray bats. For example, cave hobbyists cause problems by intruding in bat caves during hibernation. The commercializa-

tion of already limited cave sites is another problem. Pollution from pesticides and other industrial toxins and encroachment of human habitation have destroyed the habitat that produces the gray bat's food sources. In addition, dam building, irrigation, and water diversion have flooded caves through this bat's range.

Protective measures

Some progress has been made to protect this species. One step is the purchase of critical cave sites such as Sauta and New Fern Caves. Other steps include the fencing of important caves, the cooperation of various flood control agencies to regulate water management and minimize cave damage, and recent state and federal legislation aimed at protecting more bat habitats.

Indiana Bat
(Myotis sodalis)

ESA: Endangered

IUCN: Endangered

Weight: ¼ oz. (7 g)
Length: 1½–2 in. (4–5 cm), excluding tail
Diet: Flying insects
Gestation period: 60 to 90 days, after delayed fertilization
Longevity: 4–8 years
Habitat: Caves and forest near water
Range: Eastern United States

THE INDIANA BAT is a medium-sized member of the genus *Myotis* and is often mistaken for the little brown bat (*Myotis lucifu-*

gus). The Indiana bat is pinkish white, while the little brown bat is bronze. The hind feet of the Indiana bat are smaller and more delicate, and the hair on the feet and wings is shorter than that on the little brown bat.

Despite its name, the range of the Indiana bat extends over much of the eastern half of the United States. In the early 1990s the total population was estimated at fewer than 400,000 bats. The few large hibernating populations today are found in Indiana, Missouri, and Kentucky. Smaller populations or individuals have been recorded in the states of Alabama, Arkansas, Connecticut, Florida, Georgia, Illinois, Iowa, Maryland, Massachusetts, Michigan, Mississippi, New Jersey, New York, North Carolina, Ohio, Oklahoma, Pennsylvania, Tennessee, Vermont, Virginia, West Virginia, and Wisconsin. Some sightings may only represent wanderers rather than viable populations.

Approximately 85 percent of the entire known Indiana bat population winters in only seven caves, with almost one half being limited to just two of these caves. Summer nursery colonies, with 100 bats or less, have been found beneath the loose bark of trees.

Migration

Indiana bats migrate between winter and summer roosts. When the bats arrive at hibernation caves, a unique swarming occurs. Large numbers of the bats fly in and out of the caves from dusk to dawn. Few bats roost during the day, even though this is uncommon behavior for these nocturnal flyers. The swarming may last for up to two weeks, as the bats forage to stockpile fat reserves for the coming hibernation.

Indiana bats tend to hibernate in clusters of hundreds or thousands in the cave from which they swarmed, although records show a small number of individuals may occasionally move to another site. Males remain more active during swarming than females. Following the swarming period, which is around early October, the bats mate, and females then store the sperm and immediately begin hibernation. Nearly all males begin hibernating by the middle of November. After hibernation, females release the sperm they have stored, and only then become pregnant. They emerge from the cave in early April, soon followed by the males. By June or July the females give birth to a single bat. They are capable of flight within a month, and nursery colonies are established in the bark of trees. Little is known of the male's summer roosting habits.

The winter habitat of the Indiana bat requires secure caves near streams and forested vegetation. Secure in this case means free from disturbance. Each time a hibernating bat is aroused from its rest, it uses 10 to 30 days of its fat reserves. The summer habitat requires water and trees to support the insect population for the colony to feed upon.

The decline of the Indiana bat is a combination of natural events, such as falling rock and flooding, and human intervention. Since the number of roosting caves is already very limited, any disaster that ruins one cave can harm a large breeding population. Natural erosion is already collapsing some caves. As with many species, the influence of human habitation, deforestation, use of pesticides in the neighboring environment, and

The Townsend's big-eared bat has an extensive range throughout the western half of the United States. The Ozark and Virginia big-eared bats are both subspecies of this group.

human disturbance of hibernating bats all lead to their decline.

The decline of the Indiana bat is due to frequent collecting, handling, and banding of hibernating bats by biologists. This practice has now been stopped.

Since the Indiana bat was listed as an endangered species, populations have continued to decline despite cave management programs by state and federal agencies. Sometimes when caves were gated to prevent people from entering, bats were also prevented from entering. Efforts are being made to try to protect the bats' feeding habitat. Pollution needs to be kept in check, including pesticides that destroy insects that bats need. Public education is necessary to keep the recovery going, and the bats must not be disturbed during hibernation.

Ozark and Virginia Big-eared Bats

(Plecotus townsendii)

ESA: Endangered

IUCN: Vulnerable

Length: 1¾–2¾ in. (4.5–7 cm)
Weight: ½ oz. (13 g)
Diet: Insects
Gestation period: 40–70 days
Habitat: Caves
Range: Oklahoma, Arkansas, Kentucky, West Virginia, and North Carolina

BOTH THE Ozark big-eared bat (*Plecotus townsendii ingens*) and the Virginia big-eared bat (*Plecotus townsendii virginianus*), are subspecies of Townsend's big-eared bat (*Plecotus townsendii*), which has a wide range in the western half of the U.S. The Townsend's bat appears to be a sedentary species with no known migratory pattern. It is thought to use the same caves and the same roosts every year. Big-eared bats feed on small moths and other insects gleaned from foliage and caught in flight.

The Ozark bat has a small range, limited to eastern Oklahoma in Adair County, and north-central Arkansas in the counties of Washington and Marion. The Ozark bat is a medium-sized bat with large ears in excess of 1 inch (2.5 centimeters) long. The adults weigh from 5 to 13 grams. The Ozark bat can be distinguished from Townsend's bat by its color. It has orange to reddish brown fur instead of the darker brown back and tan belly of Townsend's bat.

The Ozark bat is considered endangered. Since arousing a bat from hibernation can deplete its fat reserves, humans who go into bat caves are considered the greatest threat to the Ozark bat. In December 1983, 210 of these bats were observed in Oklahoma. All but five were seen in a single cave in that county. In late May 1983, two maternity colonies were observed in that county, one with just 150 bats, the other with 62 bats. One colony site that had several hundred bats in 1960 had only four in 1983.

The habitat of the Ozark big-eared bat is protected by state and federal authorities. The limited habitat and population are monitored continuously. In the early 1990s the population of Ozark big-eared bats was esti-

mated at 1,800. The most important recovery step is to erect gates at cave entrances that prevent people entering, while allowing the bats easy access.

The Virginia big-eared bat is smaller than its Ozark cousin and can be identified by its color. Its back is a sooty brown-black instead of orange.

In Kentucky there are three Virginia big-eared bat colonies. The one in Stillhouse Cave contained about 1,000 hibernating individuals in October 1982. By 1987, there were more than 2,500. Females raise offspring in maternity caves close to food; but the site of the maternity colony is unknown. The offspring, born hairless, fly at three weeks of age and are weaned by six weeks.

Populations

Twenty hibernating Virginia big-eared bats were seen in Black Rock Cliffs Cave, North Carolina, in 1984. Before this, the species was unknown there. In Virginia, only one active colony is known. It uses Cassel Farms No. 2 Cave as a maternity colony, and Higgenbothams Cave as a hibernation cave. A 1988 census indicated that this population of several hundred individuals is stable. In West Virginia, estimates in 1996 found there were around 6,000 individuals. In 1996 a new summer colony was discovered in Grant County, West Virginia.

The Virginia big-eared bat is, however, endangered. Its habitat is protected by state and federal authorities, and its habitat and population are monitored continuously. A count in the early 1990s estimated the population at around 13,000 individuals.

George H. Jenkins

BEARS

Class: Mammalia

Order: Carnivora

Family: Ursidae

It has been suggested by some experts that conflict between humans and bears may be inevitable. Humans and bears are both omnivorous. Both are unpredictable, resist territorial confinement, occupy the highest rung in the food chain, and need fear few other creatures—except perhaps each other. Bears are like people in other ways as well, for they come in a variety of colors and sizes and live in many different climates.

The bear has many different names, such as the grizzly, the Kodiak, the sloth, and the polar bear. In color it can be gray, charcoal, brown, beige, cinnamon, blond, reddish, white, or grizzled. It can weigh as little as 500 pounds (230 kilograms) or as much as 2,000 pounds (0.9 metric ton). Many of these bears are now endangered species.

American Black Bear

(Ursus americanus)

ESA: Threatened

Weight: Males 130–660 lb. (60–300 kg); females 88–175 lb. (40–80kg)

Length: 4½–6 ft. (1.4–1.8 m)

Diet: Opportunistic omnivore: animal matter, vegetable matter

Gestation period: 220 days

Longevity: 40 or more years in captivity

Habitat: Forested areas; sea level to 8,250 feet (2,500 meters)

Range: 32 U.S. states, north-central Mexico, all provinces and territories of Canada except Prince Edward Island

THE AMERICAN black bear is the most common bear in North America with a very broad range. There are a number of subspecies, but the taxonomy is still a little confused and requires further study.

The present North American population of black bears is 400,000 to 750,000, with the highest concentrations in the northeast and the northwest. The numbers are fairly stable, except for the area around Louisiana, Mississippi, and a portion of Texas. This is the range of the subspecies *Ursus americanus luteolus*. Its environment has been severely degraded due to oil exploration and channeling of water supplies.

Muticolored black bears

Black bears, contrary to their name, come in a variety of colors. Most of the black bears found in Alaska, northern Canada, and eastern North America from Newfoundland to Florida are mostly black with tan to brown muzzles. Many have white to cream colored chest patches.

The brown color phase can be encountered in different gradations, such as cinnamon, honey, and light brown to chocolate brown. These colors are most common in the west and south of North America, but they are also found in the same areas in which black coloration occurs.

Glacier, or blue, bears (also known as gray bears) are bluish gray over the body, with many individuals showing a darker head color. They are found in a small area of northwest British Columbia and southeast Alaska.

White, or Kermode, bears are found in west-central British Columbia and adjacent islands. They are creamy white, but they are found in other colors such as bright yellow, chestnut red, bluish gray, and bright orange. The white color phase is often described as an albino, but they are not albinos, only color varia-

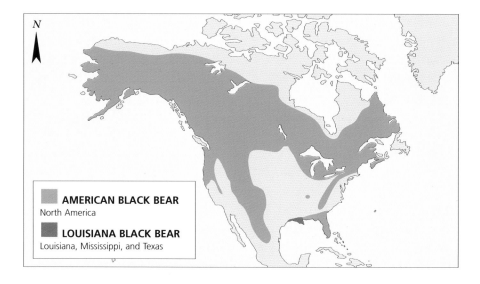

N

| | AMERICAN BLACK BEAR North America |
| LOUISIANA BLACK BEAR Louisiana, Mississippi, and Texas |

tions. All of them have brown, perfectly normal eyes.

Black bears are formidable animals and can be powerful, dangerous antagonists. They are classed as carnivores because of their dentition and lineage. However, by habit they are true omnivores. They are opportunists ready to take advantage of whatever comes their way. They will kill other animals and eat them, eat carrion, dig roots and eat berries, and also graze. Nothing edible misses their constant search for food. This endless food quest together with the continually increasing presence of tourists in their domain has resulted in a number of traumatic confrontations with humans.

Winter sleep

Black bears go into a semi-torpor, which is referred to as a hibernation. In late summer and early autumn they gorge themselves on food, creating an immense amount of fat. With the arrival of winter they find themselves a den and go into their hibernation state, during which time they live off their accumulated fat. It is not a true hibernation as is seen in some rodents because the bear can be aroused and may even leave its den and walk around.

Bears in the wild are very adaptable to changing environments. They normally have ranges that vary from 2½–10 square miles (6.5–26 square kilometers). The size of the range is relative to food supply.

Males reach reproductive maturity at four to five years of age. Females are fertile at three to four years. Mating takes place in May and June. The fertilized

egg floats free until about October when it then implants in the uterus. Delayed implantation is a common method of reproduction in bears. If by October the female has not obtained adequate fat reserves, the zygote, or fertilized embryo, will not implant and will be reabsorbed. One to four young are born, most commonly two, after a gestation period of 220 days, in January or February, while the female is still in hibernation. The young are between 8½ and 11½ ounces (240 and 330 grams) at birth. They are born blind and deaf and almost hairless, with the front legs more

A black bear cub uses its strong claws to climb a tree. Cubs become independent of their mothers after a year or more.

developed than the rear legs. The cubs will generally stay with their mother for a year or more, unless she drives them off earlier. This system results in females reproducing about every other year

Like other bears, the black bear mother fiercely defends her cubs from any danger. This includes male bears, which have been known to kill baby bears and eat them.

Warren D. Thomas

Asian Black Bear

(Ursus thibetanus)

IUCN: Vulnerable

Weight: Males, 240–330 lb.
(110–150 kg); females,
140–200 lb. (65–90 kg)
Length: 4–5¾ ft. (1.2–1.8 m)
Diet: Fruit, buds, invertebrates,
small vertebrates, carrion
Gestation period: 210–240 days
Longevity: 33 years in captivity
Habitat: Moist deciduous
forest, brushy areas in hills and
mountains
Range: Asia

THE ASIAN BLACK BEAR has traditionally lived in the mountainous elevations of Iran, Afghanistan, and Pakistan. East of the Himalayas it has ranged as far south as Bangladesh and Laos, as well as into Manchuria and other forested areas of China. It is known to exist on the island of Taiwan, as well as on the Japanese islands of Honshu and Shikoku. Often called the moon bear because of the large crescent-shaped mark on its chest, this bear is generally jet black with a tan muzzle. A short white beard and a shaggy mane encircle its round face. Its ears are large for a bear and are spaced rather far apart.

As is the case in North America, the black bears of Asia tend to be smaller than brown bears. The Asian black bear may stand to an upright height of about 6 feet (1.8 meters) and weigh about 250 pounds (115 kilograms). A particularly large male may be over 6 feet (1.8 meters) tall and weigh more than 300 pounds (135 kilograms). Females are somewhat smaller.

Two species?

Recently, an international team of researchers visited the Barun Valley of Nepal to investigate reports that there were two distinct species of black bear in the area. The smaller, younger bears were thought to be frequenting trees and eating fruits and nuts, while the larger, older bears were foraging primarily on the ground. After some study, the researchers concluded that the animals were the same species and that behavioral differences were attributable to age and weight. Not only do younger bears behave differently than older ones, but their activities also vary depending upon the environment. One constant is that bears are largely nocturnal.

Different diets

Typically, the Asian bear spends its days sleeping in a cave or hollow tree and its nights foraging for food. In India the bears are fiercely carnivorous, killing and eating sheep, goats, and cattle. They are even said to be capable of killing giant water buffalo by breaking their necks. In Mongolia, however, the bears seem much less predaceous, preferring termites, beetle larvae, honey, fruit, nuts, and berries. In Indochina the bears reportedly eat a great deal of grain.

Deforestation of habitat

Throughout most of Asia the animal suffers the consequences of deforestation and encroachment on their habitat by humans. It is increasingly scarce in those regions where it is likely to come in contact with people. In addition to cherishing bears' paws as a luxury food, many people in China believe the bear's meat, bile, and bones all have medicinal value. Scarce as the animal is in other areas of Asia, it is common in Japan, where it is sometimes seen as a destructive pest.

Thousands hunted

The Japanese black bear frequently peels the bark from valuable timber trees, permanently damaging them by gnawing the exposed pulp. On tree farms bears have been known to damage as many as 40 trees in a single night. Japanese cedar and cypress trees are especially vulnerable to the marauding animals. While these threatened black bears continue to disappear from much of Asia, they are being hunted and killed in Japan—as many as two or three thousand bears a year are thought to be destroyed there.

Black bears are nest builders. In Japanese, their nests are called *enza*. They resemble crows' nests, consisting of branches that are broken and then piled into a big wad on a secure branch. Since acorns are the Japanese bear's favorite food, a large oak tree may contain as many as six or seven *enza*. The bears use some of the larger nests for snoozing or sleeping during stormy weather.

Hibernation

Although some southern bears hibernate briefly or not at all, and others simply seek lower elevations during the cooler months, pregnant females always retreat to a den. Hollowed trees or logs are their preferred shelters. In

Japan, in the Akita district of northern Honshu, the bears hibernate in mountainous areas where the snow accumulates and remains on the ground for most of the winter. The deep snow acts as insulation and thus provides the bears with an extra measure of warmth.

Delayed birth

As with all bears, births occur many months after breeding because of delayed implantation. Characteristically, the fertilized egg does not implant in the uterine wall until several months after copulation. The fertilized ovum remains detached for several months in the female reproductive tract. About 90 days before birth, the egg attaches to the uterine wall and fetal development begins. Two to four cubs are born blind, hairless, and weighing perhaps as little as 8 ounces (227 grams). This usually occurs in late winter, shortly before the female emerges from hibernation.

Cruel exploitation?

The Asian black bear's relationship with humanity has been persistently troubled. In Japan, the bears kill an average of two or three people a year and injure as many as 30 more. Nonetheless, these bears are the most easily tamed and trained of bears. In India they are often captured and trained to ride bicycles and unicycles and to walk tightropes in circuses and public spectacles. Such performances, however, are regarded as cruel by conservation groups. However, the Indian government is reluctant to confiscate the animals and deprive their trainers of a livelihood.

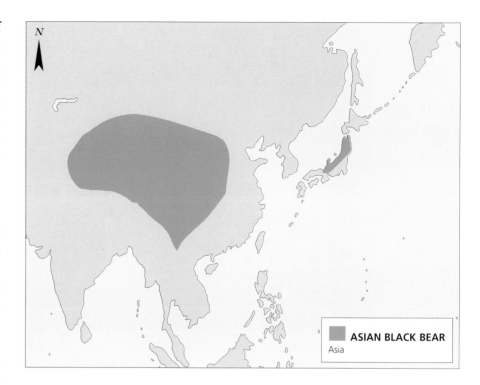

ASIAN BLACK BEAR
Asia

Brown Bear (Grizzly)

(Ursus arctos)

ESA: Threatened

Weight: Average 400 lb. (180 kg)
Length: 5½–9 ft. (1.7–2.8 m)
Diet: Omnivorous, but primarily vegetation and berries; some small vertebrates and carrion; the grizzly is known to hunt larger vertebrates
Gestation period: 180–266 days
Longevity: Average 25 years, up to 50 years in captivity
Habitat: Tundra, alpine meadows, coastlines, mountain woodlands
Range: North America, Eurasia

DURING THE EARLY years of the 20th century, naturalists were confronted by more than 80 different species and subspecies of brown bear, all of which were as similar as they were different.

While some authorities on this animal continue to recognize nine or ten subspecies, defining differences between one group of brown bear and another is generally considered less important than trying to improve their relationship with their principal antagonists: humans.

Reduced range

Once the brown bear roamed the river valleys, mountain forests, and lush meadows of the Northern Hemisphere from the Arctic Circle well down into the middle latitudes of North America, Europe, and Asia. Its range today, particularly in the United States, has been severely reduced. Most of the estimated 4,000 to 8,000 brown bears remaining in the lower 48 United States live in or near Glacier and Yellowstone National Parks (in Montana and Wyoming).

To distinguish between brown bears and black bears on the basis of color is unsatisfactory, because the brown bear can be

quite dark and the black bear can be quite brown or even blond. Examining size and features is more useful in distinguishing these two species. The brown bear is larger, has a pronounced hump on its shoulders, and has a more dish-shaped skull and face.

Particularly in North America, brown and black bears have been maligned and sentimentalized. Both have been hunted for sport, killed out of panic, and slaughtered as pests. Both have occasionally attacked, mauled, and killed human beings—even when these humans took available precautions to stay out of bear country. Although the brown bear is considered more endangered than the black bear, this may be only because its persecution has been more successful.

Dangerous bear

Bears that roam near human campsites can be unpredictable and dangerous and are to be avoided. The size of the grizzly bear makes it an intimidating sight. Most incidents of brown bear attacks occur in Alaska and Canada, where the bears are more numerous. Every year the brown bear has reportedly mauled an average of about six people in North America.

Bruce Neal, a retired Montana game warden who lived in close association with the bears for 70 years, offered his own brand of wisdom with respect to this bear. "A man is never safe for a minute in grizzly country," he

The grizzly bear has always made people nervous. Bears generally prefer to avoid people, but confrontations occur, particularly in national parks, as bears and people mix.

professed. "A lot of people think that if they don't bother the bear, it won't bother them. That's a rule that doesn't hold."

In the bear's rugged western lands, such views are common, but conservationists are inclined to point to the millions of people who frequent bear country unharmed each year, and to the number of people treated each year for dog and cat bites. The legendary Grizzly Adams, an early California settler, managed to make affectionate pets and servants of the animals, according to many witnesses.

Winter sleep

In North America, and in most countries of its range, the brown bear sleeps in a den during the cold winter months. This means that a fully developed adult must eat about 60 pounds (27 kilograms) of food each day during the warmer months. When food is scarce, brown bears will kill and eat livestock, and when they do, ranchers are inclined to retaliate. In Alaska there are no laws against killing bears, but in Montana and some other areas bears are protected by law.

In severe northern and interior climates, brown bears may den as early as September and remain in this sleeping state until April or May. But the period from November or December until March is probably a more normal period for most bears' winter sleep.

Females reproduce at age four or five and can go on reproducing for as long as 25 years. Typically, the animals breed in June or July. Although actual fetal growth takes only about 60 days, cubs are not born until about 225 days

after breeding. This is due to a method of reproduction called delayed implantation. After breeding, the embryo drifts in the female's reproductive tract without attaching to the uterine wall for several months. In this way, two to four cubs are born well into the female's winter sleep period. Blind, hairless, and weighing less than 1 pound (0.5 kilogram) each, the cubs fatten quickly on the mother's milk and may weigh 35 to 40 pounds (16 to 18 kilograms) when she emerges from hibernation, emaciated, in search of nourishment for herself and her offspring.

For the next 2½ years, the cubs will rarely wander far from their mother. Those not killed or trapped by humans, or eaten by wolves or fellow bears, are driven off by the mother before she goes into estrus; she is then ready to breed again and start another litter. Once they have been driven off, male cubs wander farther from their mother's territory than the females.

In Canada and Alaska the bears become exceedingly big and strong by feeding on high-protein grasses and salmon. Although equally expert in fishing, the brown bears of eastern Asia do not attain such size and weight. In Japan, brown bears are confined to Hokkaido, the northernmost island. This island is only about 30,000 square miles (77,700 square kilometers) in size, yet supports about four times as many brown bears as the United States does. Japanese brown bears still carry a bounty on their heads, because the Japanese government continues to view both brown and black bears as dangerous pests.

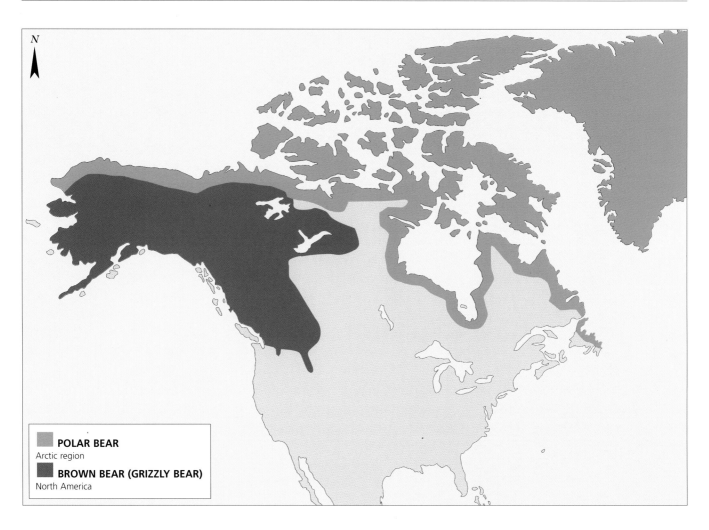

POLAR BEAR
Arctic region

BROWN BEAR (GRIZZLY BEAR)
North America

Polar Bear
(Ursus maritimus)

IUCN: Lower risk

Weight: Average 660–1,760 lb. (300–800 kg)
Length: 8½–11½ ft. (2.6–3.5 m)
Diet: Ringed seal, birds, fish, small mammals, and berries
Gestation period: 195–265 days
Longevity: 25–30 years, 30 or more years in captivity
Habitat: Pack ice, arctic coastal areas
Range: Arctic region

WHEREVER SEA ICE mixes with open water in the Northern Hemisphere, the polar bear can be found. Polar bears inhabit Russia, Norway, Greenland, Canada, and the United States. They have even been carried on ice floes as far as Iceland and northern Japan.

So strong and hardy are these bears that they have been observed swimming in icy Arctic waters about 75 miles (120 kilometers) from the nearest land, and polar bear footprints have been found within two degrees of the North Pole.

In pursuit of ringed seals, which make up the bulk of its diet, the polar bear wanders out early each winter onto vast sheets of frozen ice. In warmer weather the ice breaks up, and by swimming, riding the ice floes, and walking, the bears make their way back to their original hunting grounds.

A large white bear with a coat that often acquires a yellowish cast, the polar bear has a graceful neck and a smaller, more pointed head and snout than most bears. The outer hairs of the polar bear's coat are entirely hollow and act like individual solar collectors, absorbing the sun's rays to transfer heat to the bear's black skin. The inner hairs of the polar bear's coat are so effective at trapping infrared radiation that the presence of polar bears cannot be monitored by infrared photography, which relies on radiated heat.

Protection from the cold
Polar bears have a thick 2- to 4-inch (5- to 10-centimeter) layer of subcutaneous fat (a layer of fat beneath the skin that is lighter in

Polar bears are among the largest of all the bears, sometimes growing as long as a small compact car.

weight than bone or muscle). With their smaller heads and layers of fat, polar bears typically weigh less than comparably sized brown bears. Polar bear paws are heavily matted, tufted with short, stiff hairs that protect the bottoms of their feet from the intense cold and provide traction on ice and snow. Front paws measuring as much as 12 inches (30 centimeters) in diameter serve as weapons. They are also efficient paddles, enabling the animal to swim 50 to 60 miles (80 to 100 kilometers) at a stretch.

Close relatives

As different as they are in many respects, polar bears and brown bears have been known to crossbreed in captivity. Their offspring are also able to produce offspring, which shows how closely related these species are to one another. Many scientists believe that the polar bear evolved from the brown bear approximately 200,000 years ago.

Female polar bears stop growing after four years and weigh up to 660 pounds (300 kilograms). Males continue to grow for as long as eight years and can easily attain 1,300 pounds (590 kilograms). A full-grown male can measure 8½–11½ feet (2.6–3.5 meters). The largest polar bear ever recorded was over 12 feet (3.7 meters) and weighed 2,200 pounds (1 metric ton).

Swimming hunters

Because they are excellent swimmers, polar bears willingly enter frigid waters to catch food or escape enemies. Able to swim at about 6 miles (10 kilometers) per hour—faster than they normally walk—they can remain submerged under water for up to two minutes. Swimming at a depth of about 10–15 feet (3–4.6 meters), they sometimes hunt seabirds resting on the water's surface by coming up beneath them. They also prey on crabs and shellfish in shallow waters.

Their primary prey is the ringed seal. When stalking them on the ice, polar bears have been observed covering their black noses to reduce the chances of being seen. They are also known to ambush sleeping seals by attacking them from the water.

To conserve heat and energy, however, the bears prefer to lie in wait for seals beside breathing holes in the ice. Seals surfacing to breathe are scooped violently out of the sea by the bear's snout and are usually eaten immediately. The bears can digest as much as 150 pounds (68 kilograms) of seal meat in a matter of hours. To maintain body weight, a full-grown adult needs to eat a quantity equal to the weight of an adult seal every five or six days.

Different kinds of prey

In summer, or when seals are unavailable, the polar bear turns to caribou, musk ox, lemmings, water fowl, salmon, or even an arctic fox that ventures too close. These bears will also eat bird's eggs, fish, mushrooms, grasses, berries, and seaweed.

As many as one hundred polar bears have been spotted sharing the bounty of a single dead whale. Now and then a polar bear will risk a walrus, but this animal is a very formidable prey, and groups of walrus have been known to kill their attacker. Walrus males will eat polar bear cubs or sows as well.

After months of seal harvesting and drifting on polar ice, the bears are often reduced to walking back to their original hunting grounds. When necessary they can walk a steady 4 miles (6 kilometers) per hour; even in featureless Arctic regions they can retain an unerring sense of direction. For example, of four bears removed as potentially dangerous pests near the town of Churchill on the west coast of Hudson Bay, two returned to the area—150 air miles (240 kilometers) away—in about two weeks. During a single lifetime, polar bears have been known to wander as far as 100,000 miles (161,000 kilometers) through the open wilderness.

Birth during hibernation

Polar bears are difficult to observe in severe winter weather, so there is some disagreement about their hibernation habits. Seasonal patterns also differ from region to region. Apparently, only the breeding female dens for an extended period. Females enter estrus sometime between March and July. After fertilization the tiny embryo divides a few times, then free-floats in the uterus, not resuming development and attaching to the uterine wall until late summer or early fall. Denned females give birth in October or

November to one to four blind, hairless cubs, each weighing about 20 ounces (567 grams). In two months the suckling cubs will have gained 20 to 25 times their birth weight, weighing as much as 40 pounds (18 kilograms) when they emerge from the den. By August they will weigh 100 pounds (45 kilo-

Polar bears have many adaptations that help them survive in a harsh climate, including a 2- to 4-inch (5- to 10-centimeter) layer of fat beneath the skin. In addition, the outer hairs of this bear's fur absorb the sun's rays and transfer heat to the black skin.

grams) each. They will den with their mother for two more years, when she is ready to breed again.

Hunted bears

The beautiful pelt of the polar bear became very popular in the 20th century. It was desired more than any other mammal fur; therefore, its value to hunters made it an irresistible target. The world population of polar bears is estimated at 20,000, but their numbers are threatened by the potential exploration in the arctic habitat for more oil and natural gas. The hunting of polar bears was prohibited by the United States Marine Mammal Protection Act of 1972, but since that time the yearly worldwide kill still approaches 1,000 animals. As more people move into the once desolate northern regions to work on natural gas and petroleum fields, some experts fear the temptation to start poaching will increase, as native peoples hunt polar bears for profit.

Sloth Bear
(Melursus ursinus)

IUCN: Vulnerable

Weight: 120–320 lb. (55–145 kg)
Length: 4½–6 ft. (1.4–1.8 m)
Diet: Mostly termites; also grubs, honey, eggs, carrion, vegetation, and fruit
Gestation period: 180–210 days
Longevity: Up to 40 years in captivity
Habitat: Moist or dry forest, especially around rocky outcroppings
Range: India, Nepal, Sri Lanka

EUROPEANS BASED in India often killed sloth bears for sport, then, in the interest of science, sent their skins home for study. On the basis of their skins, snouts, and the descriptions of its behavior, early naturalists considered the animal to be a huge sloth—an entirely different species. The arrival of the first live sloth bears in Paris in the early 19th century, however, persuaded scientists to reverse this theory. They decided that they were dealing with a sloth-like bear, rather than a bear-like sloth.

Early confusion about the sloth bear is understandable. It has much in common with the true sloth—perhaps more than it shares with many bears. It also has a great deal in common with anteaters (another member of the sloth order), beginning with its fondness for ants and termites.

Unusual appearance

An adult sloth bear has a long, dirty white or gray muzzle with big, protruding, lips. These mobile lips and long snout help it to bore into termite dens and anthills and suck up its favorite foods. With the ability to open and close its nostrils at will, the sloth bear can feed without fear of being bitten and stung internally. And the sloth bear's short-haired muzzle makes it all the harder for insects to escape the bear's appetite.

Sloth bears have blunt, curved claws up to 3 inches (8 centimeters) long, useful for climbing and gripping tree branches and limbs. But they are even more suited to digging, exposing ants and termites. Typically, the bear begins to feed by breaking into the termites' hard mound, insert-

ing its long, narrow muzzle, and blowing violently. Such huffing and puffing clears away the dust and debris and exposes the insects and their larvae. The sucking and blowing noises of a feeding sloth bear are said to be audible for about 200 yards (180 meters) in the jungle.

Varied diet

Sloth bears do not live on ants and termites alone. They are particularly fond of honey and will endure considerable suffering to enjoy it. Once they secure a tree-hung honeycomb, they alternate between bites of the comb and efforts to clear their faces of stinging insects. Crying with pain, they still manage to devour every morsel of the comb. The bears are also fond of berries, sugarcane, small animals, and scavenged tiger kills. The bears even compete directly with the people of India for the fleshy flowers of the Mohwa (*Madhuca latifolia*), a blossom gobbled by the bears but used by humans to brew a sweet and potent alcoholic beverage.

Although somewhat larger than the sun bear, the sloth bear is smaller than most other bears but has a longer tail. Its tail measures about 7 inches (18 centimeters). The largest sloth bears stand upright to a height of 6 feet (1.8 meters) and measure about 3 feet (0.9 meter) when down on all fours.

Shaggy coat

The long, shaggy and unkempt black coat, with its prominent white or light-colored chevron on the chest, would seem ill-suited to the hot steamy weather that predominates in the east Indian

The sloth bear was so named by Europeans who mistakenly believed that this animal was indeed a sloth—a completely different animal.

jungles. The shaggy, parka-like mane around the animal's head and neck suggest still added discomfort. Yet the bear manages to stay cool.

Easily surprised

Primarily nocturnal, sloth bears seek to avoid human contact. They are not particularly aggressive but can be dangerous when surprised. Unfortunately, because they are noisy creatures without highly developed vision, they are rather easily startled. When this happens they may roar, become enraged, or charge the intruder. More often than not, the charge turns out to be a bluff, and the bear quickly retreats. Sometimes, however, the panicked creature will maul an intruder before retreating. Such attacks can be fatal.

Talkative bear

The sloth bear has a slow, ambling walk but can run quickly for short distances when it desires. It can climb trees and is comfortable in them, but it does not climb when afraid, preferring to leave the vicinity of the perceived threat. For a bear, it is unusually garrulous and seems to communicate by using a variety of grunts and growls.

In Sri Lanka, the bears breed year round, while in India the mating season is between April and June. Sloth bears do not hibernate, but the pregnant female dens in a cave or a shelter dug under boulders or tree roots. Two or three cubs emerge from the lair in about five weeks. They then travel through the forest on their mother's back from one feeding site to another.

Territorial marks

Sloth bears are territorial and know their territory from birth. Each cub establishes its own station on its mother's back, fighting with fellow cubs to remain there. Fully grown males later mark the trunks of trees by scraping them with their forepaws and rubbing the tree trunks with their flanks.

Somewhere between 7,000 and 10,000 of these bears are thought to exist. They live in the forested areas of Sri Lanka, on the Indian subcontinent northward to the base of the Himalayas and eastward to Assam. A few live in Nepal's Chitwan National Park. This species was very common in India as recently as two decades ago, but they have since become victims of wholesale land-clearing and deforestation.

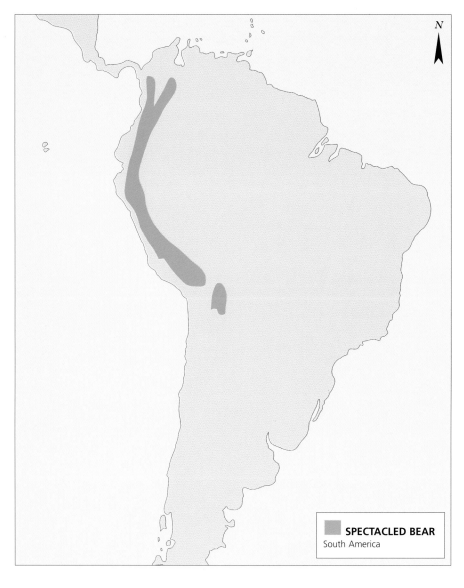

SPECTACLED BEAR
South America

Spectacled Bear

(Tremarctos ornatus)

IUCN: Vulnerable

Weight: 175–275 lb. (80–125 kg)

Length: 4–6 ft. (1.2–1.8 m)

Diet: Fruit, bromeliads

Gestation period: 195–255 days

Longevity: Approximately 30 years

Habitat: Humid forests, grasslands above 6,500 ft. (2,000 m)

Range: South America

THOUGHT TO BE the sole survivor of a species that once ranged across the Americas during the last ice age, the spectacled bear (also known as the Andean bear or the *ucumari*) is now the only bear found in South America. Perhaps as few as 2,000 still live in the wild, with another 100 living in captivity. Like most other bear species, the spectacled bear seems to prefer a wooded, mountainous habitat. Sometimes, however, it will climb above the tree line to feed on the berries and plants that grow only at the highest elevations.

Most of the remaining bears live in the Andes from Venezuela to Chile. A few inhabit the Cayambe-Coca National Park on the western slopes of the Andes Mountains in Ecuador. South American conservation efforts to protect the only known travel corridor for the bears, between the central and eastern Andean ranges, are under way. They function reasonably well despite political instabilities in the region. A committee coordinates government actions in the sanctuary at Machu Pichu in Peru.

A bear that wears glasses

Beige or tawny rings or markings that surround its tiny eyes give this bear a spectacled or masked appearance—hence its most commonly used name. Frequently these patterns are only half circles and extend downward along the animal's throat and chest. Sometimes the lighter coloration is absent altogether. For the most part, the bear is black and very shaggy, particularly around the neck and shoulders. This gives it a maned appearance and a certain resemblance to the Asian black bear. The spectacled bear has only 13 ribs, one pair less than other bears. It also has an unusually large skull, strong teeth, and powerful jaws.

This bear tends to be on the small side. A typical adult stands about 30 inches (76 centimeters) high, on all fours. Standing on its hind legs, its average upright height is about 4 to 6 feet (1.2 to 1.8 meters).

The spectacled bears' troubles with humans go back to the arrival of the Spaniards in the New World. For entertainment, the conquistadores first speared the bears from horseback, then drank their blood, believing that in this way they could acquire the animals' courage.

In modern times, bears have been considered less an index of prowess and courage than as pests. Their prodigious appetite for corn is largely responsible for this reputation. Until very recently, farmers blamed bears for devouring much of their crops and routinely poisoned them, destroying entire families in the process.

The spectacled bear eats more vegetarian food than most bears, enjoying fruit, sugarcane, corn, honey, and varieties of tough plants that other animals can't chew. Unopened palm leaves, cactus, palm nuts, bulbs, and roots of various sorts are its preferred diet. This animal is particularly fond of fruit and, as some of its favored fruits ripen and rot within a short period, it will often climbs into a tree's lower branches, alternately gorging and sleeping until the tree is entirely bare. But the spectacled bear doesn't live by fruit alone. It also eats mice, rabbits, birds, ants, llamas, and, occasionally, domestic cattle.

Fierce but extraordinarily shy, this bear prefers to travel along high ridgelines far above most human habitation, avoiding human contact wherever possible. So quickly does it travel through even the densest vegetation and undergrowth that even researchers knowing its whereabouts rarely come into contact with the animal.

The *ucumari*, or spectacled bear, lives only in the high Andes of South America. Its unusual markings give this species the appearance of wearing a mask.

At four years of age, females begin to breed. The fertilized ovum floats in the uterus for a time before attaching to the uterine wall and developing fully. In lean times, embryos are thought to be reabsorbed by the female, so that no birth actually takes place. Most births occur in January, only a few weeks before the forest fruits begin to ripen.

Females den before giving birth in the rainy season to one or two (rarely three) cubs. The nest is prepared on the ground under boulders or tree roots. There is no evidence of hibernation. Birth weights are 11 to 18 ounces (310 to 510 grams). Within a month the cubs open their eyes and begin to move about. They ride on their mother's back and hide in her fur until they become too large to be easily carried. Mother and cubs communicate with a trilling sound; cubs hum while

they nurse; and both cubs and adults screech when they feel threatened. At six to eight months of age, cubs are ready to leave their mother and live on their own.

For some time ranchers have destroyed spectacled bears suspected of preying on domestic cattle. In addition, various parts of the bear are used for their supposed medicinal properties. For example, there continues to be a lucrative market for spectacled bear organs and bear fat—a folk remedy for arthritis.

Because spectacled bears are thinly scattered over so wide a territory, and because human poverty is so widespread in their natural habitat, they are hard to protect. Regional governments are reluctant to commit needed resources to protect endangered animals while so many fundamental human needs remain unaddressed. Even the most conservation-minded governments in the region rarely prosecute poachers, whose livelihood depends on the bear. Finally, as is the case worldwide, the animals are losing their habitat to deforestation and development.

Sun Bear
(Ursus malayanus)

IUCN: Data deficient

Weight: 59–143 lb. (27–65 kg)
Length: 3¼–4½ ft. (1–1.4 m)
Diet: Omnivorous
Gestation period: 95 days
Longevity: Average 20 years
Habitat: Dense forest
Range: Malaysia, Indonesia

PREDOMINANTLY CREATURES of the Northern Hemisphere, bears may soon cease to exist altogether south of the equator. At the moment, only two species of bear are found in the southern half of the world. Both the spectacled bear and the sun bear struggle to survive a variety of destructive forces.

The relatively few remaining sun bears live in the forests of Malaysia, with a handful surviving in Java, Sumatra, Burma, and Thailand. A few also survive in northeastern India (in and around Blue Mountain in the Chimtuipui district of Mizoram), and also in the Namdhapa Tiger Preserve in the Tirup district of Arunachal Pradesh. A very few may live in Manipur, Nagaland, and Tripura. Everywhere their numbers are dwindling. The sun bear is classified by the IUCN as data deficient, which means that there is not enough information to assess the risk of extinction.

Wanderers
Since they live in the jungle far from salmon runs, berry patches, and garbage dumps favored by bears of the Northern Hemisphere, these bears must wander almost continuously in search of food. Food consists of almost anything they can come by—lizards, small birds, monkeys, eggs, berries, roots, honey, and varieties of insects. Unlike other bears, they are known to travel and forage in pairs in search of food. Such cooperation is unusual in bears.

Dr. John Paine of the World Wildlife Fund believes that more than 24,000 acres of forest are required to support a single sun bear. Yet with the dwindling of

thick equatorial forests, sun bears and other forest animals are increasingly confined to smaller environments. Habitat destruction continues to be a threat to the survival of the sun bear.

Part of the problem is economic. The sale of valuable hardwoods is a source of revenue to countries plagued by underdevelopment and poverty. Logging is big business in Borneo, for example, but large-scale deforestation there seems not only to reduce the bear's habitat, but also to bring about subtle changes in climate. Dry spells in Borneo have had an impact on what will grow there, and on what the sun bear can find to eat.

Conflict with farmers
On a more regional level, the bear's appetite for variety often leads it into destructive and one-sided conflicts with farmers and plantation owners. For example, the sun bear likes to eat the heart of coconut palms, the large, growing bud at the top of coconut trees. Since this usually kills the trees, coconut plantation owners often seek the destruction of any bear found in the vicinity of their crop.

As the world's smallest bears, sun bears have a kind of clumsy charm that attracts people with a liking for exotic pets. Although they are not teddy bears, sun bear cubs are playful and affectionate. Poachers routinely kill breeding females, capture their cubs, and sell them as pets. The cubs eventually become too strong and destructive for captivity, but the market for pet bear cubs continues to threaten the security and well-being of the animals in the wild.

Observers should not be deceived by the small size of the sun bear. It can be fierce when forced to defend itself.

Also known as a honey bear or Malay bear, the sun bear derives its name from the yellow or tawny crescent on its chest. Sometimes the crescent is small and hard to see; sometimes it does not even exist. This bear has small, beady eyes, rounded ears, and paws with long sickle-shaped claws. The muzzle may be grayish white to orange. The rest is gray and primarily hairless. The bear has short bowlegs. On the ground, it often stands upright to get a better view of its surroundings. It climbs and naps in trees and makes its bed in platforms of broken branches 6 to 24 feet (1.8 to 7.3 meters) above the ground.

Despite their size, sun bears are extremely fierce. Tigers and other carnivorous jungle animals give them a wide berth. One of the things that makes sun bears so formidable in combat is that they have very loose skin. Should a larger predator grab a bear in its mouth, the latter can twist itself loose and counterattack with its own powerful bite.

The bears do not seem to hibernate, although birthing and cooling-off dens are dug in or around tree roots and covered with leaves. After a pregnancy lasting a little over three months, females give birth to an average of two tiny, blind, and hairless cubs. The cubs weigh about 7 ounces (200 grams), but quickly put on weight and learn to walk. In three or four weeks they emerge from the den, remaining with their mother until they are fully grown and she is ready to breed again.

A survey party in Borneo made a series of disturbing discoveries. After exploration of the jungle and many conversations with residents, they found a total of only nine bears. Of those, six were less than fully grown and all were living in captivity—many as illegal pets. According to the survey, the Malaysian government occasionally confiscates these animals and releases them into the wild. As often as not, however, officials look on the killing and capturing of sun bears as merely another struggle by humans to make a living in a land of few economic opportunities.

Renardo Barden

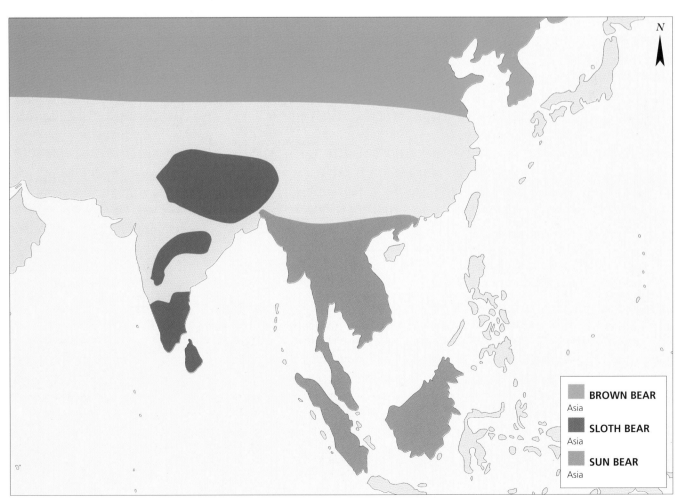

BROWN BEAR
Asia

SLOTH BEAR
Asia

SUN BEAR
Asia

BEETLES

Class: Insecta

Order: Coleoptera

The insect order Coleoptera—beetles and weevils—comprises the largest order of insects, and indeed the largest group of animals in the world. Approximately 250,000 species of beetles and weevils have been named, and perhaps many millions more remain to be described. Many of the groups of beetles contain large and conspicuous insects with brilliant metallic colors, attractive patterns, or unusual and striking forms. Thus it is not surprising that along with the butterflies and moths, beetles have proved to be one of the most commonly collected groups of insects around the world.

Beetles are found in virtually every environment on earth, from snow-capped mountaintops and arctic regions to the deepest parts of the tropics. They especially inhabit the ground and live in the soil or on it, using decaying animal or plant substances for homes. Dung, carrion, refuse, humus, rotting wood, and fungi are habitats for numerous beetle species. Approximately one-half of the beetle families has species that live under tree bark. Many other species eat living plants, and their larvae live in or on flowers, fruits, leaves, stems, or roots. A relatively small percentage of the total number of beetle species is parasitic on other insects; however, many are predators. At least a dozen families are true aquatic insects, while several other families have aquatic or semiaquatic representatives.

As with other groups, more individuals and fewer species are found in temperate regions, while more species and fewer individuals of each species are found in the Tropics. Most endangered species of beetles that have been listed are from temperate and subtropical areas, because most beetle experts tend to live in the temperate zones.

Beetles, like other insects, have three body regions: the head, thorax, and abdomen. Six legs and two pairs of wings are attached to the thorax. Beetles can generally be distinguished from other insects by their elytra, the hardened first pair of wings that cover the membranous second pair of wings, if present, that are used for flight. The largest beetles in the world measure about 6¼ inches (16 centimeters), while the smallest are about ⅕ inch (0.5 millimeter) long.

A large order

The order Coleoptera is divided into more than 100 families. These families range from one extreme to the other in species diversity. For example, the family Cephaloidae (false longhorn beetles) has only 11 species in Eastern Asia and North America, while the huge family Curculionidae (the weevils) has more than 30,000 species and a worldwide distribution. The number of beetle species listed as endangered is a minute fraction of those that must be endangered today, especially in the tropical rain forest where extensive clearing and habitat destruction are occurring at an unprecedented rate. The following are a few examples of threatened beetle species around the world, together with characteristics of their family.

Ground beetles

Members of the family Carabidae are commonly known as ground beetles. They are characterized by a rather primitive, generalized body form with a flattened, oval body that is usually dark and shiny. The larvae and adults are predatory. With about 20,000 species in worldwide distribution, this is a large family. The delta green ground beetle, *Elaphrus viridis*, is a predator that hunts springtails (order Collembola), which are small, soft-bodied insects that live at the margin of vernal pools in the Sacramento River delta of California.

One of the most restricted beetles in the world is the tooth cave ground beetle, *Rhadine persephone*. This reddish brown beetle reaches a maximum size of only ⅓ inch (8 millimeters) and, because it is adapted to caves, it has only rudimentary eyes. It is known to be found in only two small caves in the Edwards Limestone Formation in Texas. Tooth Cave is approximately 100 feet (30 meters) in length but contains a greater diversity of fauna than any other cave in Texas, with over 48 species of wildlife in it. The other known habitat of this beetle is the Kretschmarr Cave, which is about 50 feet (15 meters) deep. The Tooth Cave ground beetle is thought to feed on eggs of cave crickets (order Orthoptera). Because cave species are dependent on a regular infiltration of pure groundwater, any pollution such as sewage, pesticides, or fertilizer residue contamination could easily destroy the habitat that supports this unusual beetle.

Cave adaptations

The mold beetle family Pselaphidae also contains a rare species in Kretschmarr Cave, *Texamaurops reddelli*, the Kretschmarr Cave mold beetle. This species is less than 3 millimeters in length. It lacks eyes and is the most highly cave-adapted species of its family in Texas, perhaps even in the entire United States. This species is believed to be omnivorous but probably depends on fungus for the bulk of its diet. Expansion of the city of Austin will probably result in development of the area near the caves in the Edwards Limestone Formation. Even water pipeline construction nearby could collapse the caves or weaken them.

Tiger beetles

Tiger beetles, Cicindelidae, are favored by collectors because of their bright and varied color patterns. They are day-active predators that hunt small insects and arthropods. Larvae of tiger beetles live in burrows and are voracious predators. Both life stages appear to favor sandy soils. The Columbia River tiger beetle, *Cicindela columbica*, was formerly associated with three river systems in the Pacific Northwest of the United States, where it lived on sandbars. However, dam construction has subsequently flooded most of its former habitat. The last known colonies, in Idaho, are threatened by proposed dams. The Puritan tiger beetle, *C. puritana*, and the northeastern tiger beetle, *C. dorsalis dorsalis*, are associated with beach habitats. Both of these beetles were formerly more widespread in coastal areas of New England and the Middle Atlantic states, but human encroachment and habitat alteration have restricted their present distributions to a fraction of their historical ranges.

American burying beetle

One of the most disastrous declines ever recorded for an insect is the story of the Ameri-

This beetle, *Calosoma sycophanta*, is from the Atlas Mountains. Here, it has made a meal out of a caterpillar.

The Kretschmarr Cave mold beetle is less than three millimeters in length and is highly adapted to cave life. It is found near the Kretschmarr Cave complex in Austin, Texas.

can burying beetle, *Nicrophorous americanus*, of the family Silphidae (carrion beetles). This is a large, shiny black beetle with distinctive orange and red markings on the wing covers. Its red antennae have orange clubs. It is the largest member of its genus, measuring from 1 to 1¼ inches (2.5 to 3.2 centimeters). This beetle was once found in 32 states and three Canadian provinces, with its range extending from Nova Scotia and Quebec, south to Florida, and west to Texas and the Great Plains. Today, it is known from only two populations: one on a New England island and the other in eastern Oklahoma. The cause of this disastrous loss is unknown, although widespread use of the insecticide DDT between 1945 and 1970, as well as other pesticides, is considered a strong possibility.

The beetle is attracted to carrion (dead and decaying flesh) by smell. A nocturnal species, many of them may arrive at a carcass and fight there among themselves until one pair, usually the largest male and female, takes possession and buries the carrion. They then construct a breeding chamber. The female lays eggs on the carrion and both she and her mate remain with the eggs until they hatch, when they proceed to tend the larvae. After about 50 days, the larvae emerge as adults, and both parents and young disperse. Without parental attention, the larvae do not survive.

During the winter, adults burrow in the soil where they remain until spring. Originally, the American burying beetle apparently preferred mature, virgin forest, with deep humus and topsoils suitable for burying carrion. Thus the clearing of much of the eastern deciduous forests undoubtedly contributed to the decline of this species. This beetle is listed as critically endangered by IUCN–The World Conservation Union.

Hawaiian beetles

The archipelago of the Hawaiian Islands contains a number of species of beetles thought to be threatened, including 17 species of *Eopenthes* (Hawaiian click beetles), 72 species in the weevil genus *Proterhinus*, and 22 species of Hawaiian snout beetles in the genus *Rhyncogonus*. *Eopenthes* are members of the family Elateridae, which contains about 7,000 species worldwide. These beetles can leap when lying on their back and usually make a clicking sound when they do, hence their common name of click beetles. The adults and larvae are plant feeders. Weevils are members of the huge family Curculionidae, also commonly referred to as snout beetles due to their characteristic snout. The Kauai flightless stag beetle, *Apterocychus honoluluensis*, belongs to the family Lucanidae (stag beetles), comprising some 900 species worldwide.

Scarab beetles

The scarab beetles of the family Scarabaeidae are highly variable in color, size, and habits, with about 20,000 species widely distributed throughout the world. Most of the species feed on dung, carrion, or other decaying matter in the larval and adult stages. Some of the largest and most spectacular beetles in the world are in the Scarabaeidae family, including several subspecies of the Hercules beetle (*Dynastes hercules hercules* and *D. hercules reidi*), which in the past were considered endangered but are currently not evaluated. This means that there is insufficient accurate information on the current status of these subspecies, but it is still possible they are endangered. This situation is true of many other beetle species.

Research needed

In Florida, the three following species of scarab beetle once considered endangered are now no longer listed by IUCN–The World Conservation Union or by the United States Fish and Wildlife Service (U.S.F.W.S). More research is needed to assess the current status of these beetles. *Aphodius aegrotus* or *A. geomysi* is found in the burrows of pocket gophers, *Geomys pinetis*. This beetle feeds on pocket gopher dung and has several modifications similar to cave animals, such as reduced eyes and pigment and elongate setae (hairs). Another scarab, *Ataenius sciurus*, lives in nests of fox squirrels, *Sciurus niger*, and is probably a dung feeder. This beetle is found in north and central Florida. A third endangered species, *Ataenius woodruffi*, is known only from a single specimen collected at Flagler Beach, in Flagler County, Florida. It was collected in a mosquito light trap in an eastern beach area that is rapidly being modified by land development and the misuse of insecticides, as well as being exposed to the usual tides and storms that prevail. Nothing is known of this beetle's behavior or habitat requirements.

Longhorn beetles

One of the more beautiful species of beetles in California is the valley elderberry longhorn beetle, *Desmocerus californicus dimorphus*. Larvae are internal borers of elderberry, *Sambucus* sp., trees and shrubs in the Central Valley of California. Elderberry commonly grows in habitats along streams, creeks, and rivers.

However, nearly 99 percent of this habitat has been converted to agricultural or urban uses. To the south, in the Mojave Desert, the Mojave rabbitbush longhorn beetle, *Crossidius mojavensis mojavensis*, feeds on rabbitbush and other desert composites. It was formerly known from five locations, but it is found today in only a single locality. Both of these species of beetles are members of the longhorn beetle family, Cerambycidae, which contains many brightly colored species. The larval stages of development are usually wood-boring and sometimes cause tree damage.

Bleak future

With about 25,000 species in worldwide distribution, many additional species of wood-boring beetles, especially those that specialize in certain tree species, may expect to be threatened with extinction in the future as forest clearing continues.

Richard A. Arnold

Below is a selection of beetle species recognized as vulnerable or endangered by IUCN–The World Conservation Union.

Common name	Scientific name
Blind cave	*Glacicavicola bathysciodes*
Cerambyx longicorn	*Cerambyx cerdo*
Columbia River tiger	*Cicindela columbica*
Cresent dune scarab	*Aegialia crescenta*
Gammon's riffle	*Stenelmis gammoni*
Giulianis's dune scarab	*Pseudocotalpa giulianii*
Goldstreifiger	*Buprestis splendens*
Hermit	*Osmoderma eremita*
Lichen weevil	*Gymnopholus lichenifer*
Oahu nesiotes weevil	*Deinocossonus nesiotes*
Puritan tiger	*Cicindela puritana*
Rosalia longicorn	*Rosalia alpina*
Sacramento	*Anthicus sacramento*
San Joaquin dune	*Coelus gracilis*

The following are recognized as critically endangered by IUCN–The World Conservation Union.

Common name	Scientific name
American burying	*Nicrophorus americanus*
Cromwell chafer	*Prodontria lewisi*
Delta green ground	*Elaphrus viridis*

Beira

(Dorcatragus megalotis)

IUCN: Vulnerable

Class: Mammalia
Order: Artiodactyla
Family: Bovidae
Tribe: Neotragini
Weight: 33–55 lb. (15–25 kg)
Shoulder height: 20–25½ in. (50–65 cm)
Diet: Leaves, shoots, and twigs
Gestation period: Unknown
Longevity: Unknown
Habitat: Rocky, barren mountain areas
Range: Somalia, Djibouti, and possibly adjacent Ethiopia

THE BEIRA IS A little-known antelope that lives only in Somalia, Djibouti, and perhaps portions of Ethiopia. It has rarely been described by naturalists, and there are no well-documented studies of it in the wild. It lives in scrub brush and around rocky outcroppings in mountain areas. Its habits are similar to those of the klipspringer, which is a small Nigerian antelope.

The beira is a little animal. Only the males have horns, which are 3 to 4 inches (7 to 10 centimeters) long. They have very large ears. When alert, with ears forward, the beira's small horns become almost hidden; from a distance it is not easy to tell male from female. The beira also has an unusual foot struc-

One of the beira's primary means of protection is its curious colorations, which act as camouflage, allowing the beira to blend in well with its background. A beira can stand out in the open and virtually disappear.

ture, with a rubbery, flexible pad on the hoof that allows it to run over rocky outcroppings with surefootedness. This pad also protects the hooves from rapidly wearing down on the rocky terrain that is the beira's home.

It is rare to see one or two beira together, but there have been reports of small groups of up to 12. Beiras seem to locate a favorite spot that they consider home, and no matter how harassed or disturbed, they keep coming back to that spot. Thus, once located by a predator, their future location is predictable.

There has never been a beira known in captivity in the Western Hemisphere, but some have been captured for private collections in the Middle East. Little is known about their habits, and no quantitative data is available to assess

BEIRA
Africa

▢ Former Range
▢ Present Range

them in the wild. The beira's position is more vulnerable given its distribution in an area of civil war and expanding human and livestock populations.

Warren D. Thomas

Belorybitsa (Inconnu)

(Stenodus leucichthys leucichthys)

IUCN: Endangered

Class: Actinopterygii
Order: Salmoniformes
Family: Salmonidae
Length: 31–47 in. (80–120 cm)
Reproduction: Egg layer
Habitat: Caspian Sea, large rivers for spawning
Range: Caspian Sea basin

PRIZED FOR ITS GREAT value as a food resource, the belorybitsa, a subspecies of whitefish, is found only in the basin of the Caspian Sea. Although once very abundant, it is now rare and is considered to be endangered. Most of its life is spent in the open waters of the Caspian Sea, a saltwater environment. To reproduce, the belorybitsa must change its bodily functions so that it may enter the fresh water of the large rivers in which it spawns. The majority of Caspian belorybitsa ascend the Volga River; a small number travel up the Ural River, and a few rare specimens have been found in the Terak River. They are not found in any other rivers that drain into the Caspian Sea.

Vast harvests

These fish were harvested in great numbers in the early 1900s, when catches of up to 3 million pounds were common. During the 1950s, however, environmental changes resulted in the current ecological conditions of the Volga River. Obstructions by dams and hydroelectric power plants, and pollution by wastewater and petroleum products, caused a dramatic decline in the abundance of the belorybitsa. By 1959, less than 1,000 pounds were harvested by commercial fishing efforts of the former Soviet Union. A fishing ban was established that continues today.

The belorybitsa reaches a length of over three feet (0.9 meter) as an adult and weighs up to 30 pounds (13.5 kilograms). It is similar in appearance to its cousins the salmon and trout, but it is always silvery white and has no spots, and it never acquires the spectacular spawning colors of trout and salmon. It possesses a deeply forked tail, a small adipose fin, and small bristle-like teeth. It is long and slender and has large scales which give the fish its silvery image.

In the Caspian Sea, the belorybitsa feeds on small fish such as shad, gobies, silversides, and roach. It ceases to feed once it enters the river to spawn. Russian researchers observed that there is also a significant decrease in the fat content of the flesh associated with its entry into fresh water.

The females begin their first migration in late fall at the age of six or seven, and those that survive return to the Caspian Sea, stay for two years, and return to spawn a second time at age eight or nine. The maximum age for the belorybitsa is nine years for females and eight years for males.

Spawning

Spawning takes place above gravel, and clean flowing water is needed to incubate the eggs. After about 180 days the small fry emerge. This continues from March through April. The fry

descend the Volga with the downward flow of the powerful river; by June they begin to arrive in the Caspian Sea. Although some fish are observed to spend up to three years in lakes and backwaters in the lower reaches of the Volga, most of the young enter the world's largest inland sea within a few months after hatching. They remain in the Caspian Sea until they reach sexual maturity, then migration begins and they journey back to their original hatching ground.

Raised at hatcheries

Because of their historic importance as a food resource, efforts have been made to raise these fish in hatcheries along the Volga River. Fish are captured below the site of the Volgagrad dam and are artificially spawned. Fertilized eggs are taken to a hatchery to be incubated and hatched. Young fish are held for a few months and fed an artificial diet then released into the lower reaches of the Volga. From there they find their way to the Caspian Sea. Although this has increased the number of belorybitsa to some extent, they are not plentiful enough to allow fishing to resume, and they remain a species whose long-term survival may be in jeopardy.

Donald S. Proebstel

BETTONGS

Class: Mammalia

Order: Marsupialia

Family: Macropodidae

Bettongs belong to the same family that includes kangaroos and wallabies—56 species in all. They are marsupials, which is a much larger group of species that includes possums, koalas, numbats, and wombats. Marsupials are unique because the females have a reproductive system that is unlike that of any other mammal. They lack a true placenta, the tissue that normally passes nutrients to a growing embryo in the womb.

Females have a pouch as part of their abdomen, and they use this to carry their young. New marsupials are born after a short gestation period; they are extremely small, almost no larger than embryos.

The family that includes bettongs is confined to a small portion of the world. They are found only in Australia, New Guinea, and some of the nearby islands such as Tasmania.

Continental drift, which is the gradual moving of the continents on the earth's crust, probably explains the marsupials' evolutionary isolation.

Brush-tailed Bettong

(Bettongia penicillata)

IUCN: Lower risk

Weight: 2½–3½ lb. (1.1–1.6 kg)

Head-body length: 11–18 in. (28–46 cm)

Diet: Primarily herbivorous, some meat and carrion

Gestation period: 21 days

Longevity: 4–6 years

Habitat: Grassland, dry forest

Range: Australia

ALSO KNOWN AS rat kangaroos because they look so much like common rats, bettongs are really small marsupials. The brush-tailed bettong has sleek gray-brown fur, small rounded ears, a pinkish nose, and rows of black hair on its tail, which earned this bettong the appellation brush-tailed. Like the kangaroo, the bettong has longer hind legs than forelegs, enabling it to hop. Although not especially fast, bettongs are quite agile.

Although bettongs look similar to large rats, they are not rodents, but marsupials. They have long hind legs suitable for hopping.

During the day, most bettongs hide in nests in the shelter of a tussock or bush. These nests are made of grass and other materials carried to the nest site in the curled-up tip of the tail. Coming out by night to forage for food, bettongs wander over large home ranges, which average 83 acres (33 hectares) for males and 57 acres (23 hectares) for females. If a bettong encounters a predator, it flees with its head down and its brush tail raised. This behavior may serve to attract the predator's attention to the wrong end of its intended prey.

The bettong's diet is varied and includes mushrooms, roots, berries, tubers, and worms. Mushrooms, which are dug up with the strong claws of the forefeet, are low in protein yet make up a large proportion of its diet. The bettong cannot digest mushroom tissue, so it has gut bacteria to process them. It gains nutritional value from the bacteria and their wastes. This is symbiosis: living together in a mutually beneficial way.

Brush-tailed bettongs defend the areas near their nests from other animals and predators.

The gestation period for the brush-tailed bettong is 21 days. This period can be much longer if the embryo has to wait its turn

to enter the pouch. This waiting is known as embryonic diapause, when the embryo can be held in an arrested state of development until an older sibling leaves the pouch. The single baby weighs only 0.3 gram at birth. It crawls inside its mother's pouch, where it attaches to and suckles from one of four teats. Leaving the pouch after 115 days, the young bettong continues to suckle for another month or so. It shares the nest with its mother until it is just over six months old, when it becomes sexually mature. If it is female, it can bear young every 120 to 130 days throughout its four to six-year life span.

The brush-tailed bettong lives in grassy woods or dense brush in southwest Australia. There have been recent reintroductions of the species to several islands off the south coast of Australia.

Bettongs have often been poisoned by farmers, who consider them a threat to crops. Deforestation and the introduction of foxes and rabbits have been a problem, but this bettong is now considered to be lower risk.

Burrowing Bettong

(Bettongia lesueur)

IUCN: Vulnerable

Weight: 2–3⅓ lb. (1.1–1.5 kg)
Head-body length: 11–16 in. (28–40.5 cm)
Diet: Herbivorous
Gestation period: 21 days
Habitat: Grassland, dry forest
Range: Islands off Australia

THE HABITS OF THE small rat kangaroo known as the burrowing bettong are quite different from its close relative, the brush-tailed bettong. Its name derives from the fact that when topside vegetation is scarce, this bettong nests in underground burrows. These burrows can form maze-like colonies with over 100 separate entrances and up to 60 individuals. Even though the burrows are interconnected, studies indicate that only one male along with several females occupy a given section of a burrow. It is as yet unclear whether males compete to defend a territory, which includes a burrow system and the females within, or whether they simply defend the females. Females occasionally establish a territory from which they exclude other females.

Besides its burrowing activities, there is another behavioral difference between the burrowing bettong and the brush-tailed bettong. The burrowing bettong is entirely bipedal, never using its forefeet, even at a slow gait. Physically, it looks much like its closest surviving relative, the woylie, except that the fur is much softer and the dark-haired tail is thick with fatty deposits.

A typical gestation takes about 21 days, at which time a single youngster weighing only 0.3 gram emerges and crawls to its mother's pouch to attach to a teat. After about 115 days, the juvenile leaves the pouch, and even though neither sex reaches adult size until around 280 days, female bettongs can start to bear young at 200 days.

Because the young of bettongs and other marsupials spend so much time in the pouch com-

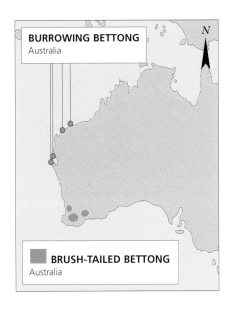

pared to the time spent in the womb, we often see a delay in the gestation process known as embryonic diapause. If a female gets pregnant again after giving birth, the embryo is held in an arrested state of development, then takes its turn for nourishment in the pouch when its older sibling leaves. At that point, it resumes development and will be born, with the period from fertilization to birth having been extended to about four months.

Once the most common mammal on the continent of Australia, the burrowing bettong can now be found only on the Barrow, Bernier, Boodie, and Dorre Islands off the coast of Western Australia.

The burrowing bettong's decline is partly attributed to competition for food and burrows with rabbits and to predation by foxes. Both of these non-native species were introduced by European settlers. In addition, even though there are viable, well-protected populations, direct killing and habitat destruction by humans have severely threatened this species.

Terry Tompkins

Greater Bilby

(Macrotis lagotis)

IUCN: Vulnerable

Class: Mammalia
Order: Marsupialia
Family: Thylacomyidae
Weight: ⅔–3½ lb. (0.3–1.6 kg)
Head-body length: 8–22 in. (20–56 cm)
Diet: Largely carnivorous
Gestation period: 14 days
Longevity: 7 years in captivity
Habitat: Dry woodland, savanna, grasslands, and desert
Range: Nothwestern and central Australia

THE GREATER BILBY is also called a rabbit-eared bandicoot, due to its long ears, its method of locomotion (it hops along like a rabbit), and its digging of burrows for its home. Bandicoots and bilbies, as members of the marsupial order, carry their young in pouches, just like the better-known marsupials such as kangaroos, wallabies, and koala bears. The greater bilby's range once covered arid and semi-arid areas of Australia, but since the arrival of European settlers, the animals have declined and are now classified as endangered.

The greater bilby has soft, fawn-gray body fur, which extends onto the base of the tail. The front half of the tail is covered with black hair, while the other half is white. Its underside is covered in soft white fur, and its forefeet have three long, powerful claws for digging. The long hind foot is covered with hair.

While solitary, bilbies do sometimes live in neighboring burrows, and they may take over deserted rabbit warrens. They are powerful diggers, building long, spiraling tunnels up to 6 feet (1.8 meters) deep and 9 feet (2.7 meters) long, with an entrance that can be closed off by tussocks or shrubs in hot daytime weather. During colder weather, bilbies often stay near their burrow entrance to keep warm and be on the alert for danger. The occupants of one burrow might consist of a male and a female, occasionally with other females but never with other males. Bilbies rarely lie down to sleep, but squat on their hind legs and tuck the snout between their forelegs.

Another distinctive feature of bilbies is their reproductive cycle. Like other bandicoots (but unlike the rest of the marsupial family), they form a placenta that attaches to the uterine wall. They also exhibit an accelerated gestation period and the babies mature quickly in the pouch. Bilbies have a 14-day gestation period, 1½ days longer than that of the long-nosed bandicoot (*Perameles nasuata*). Tiny when born (weighing less than 0.05 gram), they travel from the birth canal to the pouch, attach to a teat, and remain there for 75 to 80 days until weaned. Their life span in the wild is unknown; in captivity it is over seven years. Fully grown, greater bilbies range from 8 to 22 inches (20 to 56 centimeters) long and weigh between ⅔ and 3½ pounds (0.3 and 1.6 kilograms).

The nocturnal marsupial known as the bilby appears to have a mixture of physical traits from several different species.

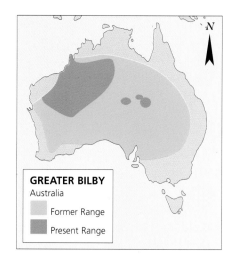

GREATER BILBY
Australia

Former Range

Present Range

Bilbies are nocturnal animals, and they are largely carnivorous. They also eat a mixture of ants, termites, beetles, larvae, seeds, fruits, mushrooms, and occasionally small vertebrates.

Because the greater bilby is so rare, it is difficult to study its habits or to guess what caused its decline. Aborigines, present in the Australian desert long before Europeans and their animals arrived, hunted bilbies for their meat and fluffy tails. Many scientists believe that the introduction of foxes and rabbits brought about the decline. The rabbit is a competitor for some of the same foods as the bilby. Other experts say that changes in climate and increased use of land for farming could have caused the disappearance of the greater bilby.

Terry Tompkins

BIRD'S-BEAK

Class: Magnoliopsida

Order: Scrophulariales

Family: Scrophulariaceae

Bird's-beak is a member of the snapdragon family, Scrophulariaceae, and is named for the hooked upper lip of the club-shaped flower, which looks like the beak of some birds. The genus name comes from the Greek roots *kordyle* (club) and *anthos* (flower). *Cordylanthus* species are hemiparasitic, which means that they make their own food by photosynthesis, but they obtain water and nutrients from the roots of other plants. This habit lets them grow and bloom later in the season when it is hot and dry and most annuals have died. Most of the nearly 40 species are found in dry areas of western North America, although two endangered species frequent salt marshes.

Palmate-bracted Bird's-beak

(Cordylanthus palmatus)

ESA: Endangered

IUCN: Vulnerable

Flowers: Purplish or cream with two lips extending from a funnel-shaped bloom

Seed capsule: Contains 14–18 brownish seeds

Leaves: Oblong with toothed margins (edges)

Height: 4–12 in. (10–30 cm)

Life cycle: Annual

Blooming period: May–October

Pollination: Bumblebees

Habitat: Terrestrial and aquatic

Range: Sacramento Valley and San Joaquin Valley, California

The name *Cordylanthus* means "club-shaped flower," while *palmatus* refers to the hand-like shape of the leaf-like floral bracts, which nearly hide the flowers. The outer bracts are green; the inner lavender bracts are deeply divided into finger-like segments. This plant is branched and covered with short, glandular hairs that excrete salt crystals, giving the mature plant a gray-green hue. All *Cordylanthus* species are hemiparasitic. The host plant for palmate-bracted bird's-beak is believed to be *Distichlis spicata*, or saltgrass. Deep roots, hemiparasitism, and salt excretion enables this bird's-beak to grow during the hot, dry months when other annuals die.

Each plant may produce as many as 1,000 seeds, but the number of plants varies annually and depends upon precipitation and other environmental factors. Seeds of *C. palmatus* float, and their dispersal is dependent upon water. They must survive periods of dormancy, for the unpredictable weather in the region may create more than one consecutive year of unsuitable conditions for germination. In a greenhouse, seeds up to four years old have germinated.

Palmate-bracted bird's-beak grows in areas of high alkalinity (pH 7–9) and salinity, with a dense clay subsoil layer that slows water penetration and groundwater movement. Germination is the most delicate stage in the life

Palmate-brachted bird's-beak manages to survive in hot and dry conditions.

cycle of a plant, and *C. palmatus* may depend on the flooded winter period as a time favorable for germination and survival. The plant community in which it grows is scrub, with sparse vegetation. It is found mainly along the edges of drainage ditches and channels, and also grows in grassy sites and alkali scalds (barren areas with a salty surface crust). This plant is a halophyte (salt lover), and it is found in association with other halophytes such as saltgrass, glasswort, seepweed, and iodine bush. The major threat to the species seems to be land conversion to agricultural and urban uses, off-road vehicle use, road maintenance, pollution, and changes in water flow or soil on nearby lands.

The existing legal protection does not appear sufficient to save the species, however.

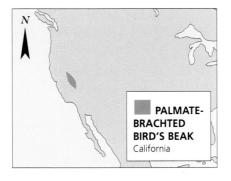

N

PALMATE-BRACHTED BIRD'S BEAK
California

Pennell's Bird's-beak

(Cordylanthus tenuis capillaris)

ESA: Endangered

IUCN: Endangered

Flowers: Tubular corolla is ½ in. (1.5 cm) long and garnet-brown (paler on the top). The floral bracts are three-lobed up to two-thirds of their length, with fine marginal hairs.
Seed capsule: Each capsule contains 10 to 16 seeds
Leaves: Narrow with smooth margins
Height: 12–16 in. (30–40 cm)
Life cycle: Annual
Blooming period: June–August
Pollination: Bees
Habitat: Chaparral
Range: San Francisco Bay, California

PENNELL'S BIRD'S-BEAK is a branching herbaceous annual of the snapdragon family with yellow-green, hairless stems and foliage that becomes purplish with age. The three-lobed outer bracts of the plant distinguish it from its nearest relative (*C. tenuis ssp. brunneus*) and from *C. pilosus*, another *Cordylanthus* found in the area. Another characteristic is that *C. pilosus* is densely hairy. All of the species are hemiparasitic.

The range of this species is limited to serpentine soils near San Francisco Bay in California. Most serpentine soils are easily eroded and inhospitable for the growth of most plants. Nevertheless, some plants, such as Pennell's bird's-beak, have adapted to the inhospitality of serpentine soils, which vary in soil chemistry, texture, and water availability. This variability and the variety of micro-climates in the San Francisco Bay region have a profound effect upon the local flora. In some areas, soil development is minimal and parent rock is extensively exposed. These serpentine barrens support a distinctive community composed of only a few species, usually growing at low densities.

Distribution and protection

Pennell's bird's-beak is known at two locations, one just north of Occidental in western Sonoma County and another a few miles to the west. A third population may occur on property adjacent to the second location, but permission for botanical surveys has always been refused.

The growing human population of the San Francisco Bay region and the accompanying habitat destruction is the greatest threat to this species. Serpentine habitats, because of their sparse vegetation, are especially likely to be subject to disturbances. Construction of roads, houses, recreational facilities, and waste disposal sites reduced serpentine habitat by nearly 20 percent between 1980 and 2000.

Habitat destruction also increases the fragmentation of rare plant populations, increasing the risks of extinction due to fire, pest or disease outbreaks, reproductive failure, or other natural or human-caused disasters. Plants restricted to a certain soil type and having small populations, such as Pennell's bird's-beak, may have low genetic variability. As a result, populations that become subdivided by

Pennell's bird's-beak has reddish brown flowers and grows sparsely in the dry chaparral areas of San Francisco Bay.

alterations in habitat from road construction and urbanization or from catastrophes such as disease, fire, or drought may be at high risk of genetic changes that decrease their survival ability.

Pedestrian and off-road vehicle traffic, garbage dumping, roadside spraying and mowing, and changes in the pattern of wildland fires all place a strain on wildlands. Competition with introduced species is a serious threat to serpentine natives.

The listing of these species as endangered or threatened publicizes their rarity and can make them attractive to researchers or collectors of rare plants.

Rick Imes

N

PENNELL'S BIRD'S-BEAK
California

GLOSSARY

actinopterygii: the Latin scientific name for fish

albino: any organism lacking color in the skin or fur; albino species have pink eyes, while albino fish often have no functioning eyes

amphibia: the Latin scientific name for amphibians

apically: relating to, or situated at the apex

arboreal: living in or adapted for living in trees; arboreal animals seldom, if ever, descend to the ground (see terrestrial)

arthropoda: the Latin scientific name for crustaceans and spiders

aves: the Latin scientific name for birds

barbels: a slender growth on the mouths or nostrils of certain fishes, used as a sensory organ for touch

bipedal: any organism that walks on two feet

bract: a leaf at the base of a flower stalk in plants

buff: in bird species, a yellow-white color used to describe the plumage

calyx: the green outer whorl of a flower made up of sepals

captive breeding: any method of bringing several animals of the same species into a zoo or other closed environment for the purpose of mating; if

successful, these methods can increase the population of that species

carnivore: any flesh-eating animal

carnivorous: flesh eating

carrion: the decaying flesh of a dead organism

class: a biological ranking of animals who share a common set of traits, below the rank of phylum and above the rank of order

classification: how a species is ranked biologically in relation to other species (see taxonomy)

clear cutting: a method of harvesting lumber that eliminates all the trees in a specific area rather than just selected trees

clutch, clutch size: the number of eggs laid during one nesting cycle

contiguous: touching, meeting, joining at a surface or border; the home of an animal is contiguous if it is uninterrupted by natural or artificial boundaries

corolla: the separate petals, or the fused petals of a flower

cotyledon: the first leaf developed by the embryo of a seed plant

deciduous: dropping off, falling off during a certain season or at a regular stage

of growth; deciduous trees shed their leaves annually

decurved: curving downward; a bird's beak is decurved if it points toward the ground

defoliate: to strip trees and bushes of their leaves

deforestation: the process of removing trees from a particular area

diurnal: active during the day; some animals are diurnal, while others are active at night (see nocturnal)

dominance: the ability to overpower the behavior of other individuals; an animal is dominant if it affects others of its own species in a way that benefits itself; also, the trait of abundance that determines the character of a plant community: grasses dominate a prairie, and trees dominate a forest

dorsal: pertaining to or situated on the back of an organism; a dorsal fin is on the back of a fish

ecology: the study of the interrelationship between a living organism and its environment

ecosystem: a community of animals, plants, and bacteria and its interrelated physical and chemical environment

endangered species: any species on the verge of becoming extinct; disap-

pearing from the wild forever

endemic: native to a particular geographic region

estrous: the time period when female mammals can become pregnant

exotic species: a plant or animal species that is not native to its habitat

extinct species: any species that has not been located in the wild for 50 years and is presumed to have disappeared forever

family: a biological ranking of species that share specific traits, below the rank of order and above genus; subfamily is a narrower classification of species in the same family

feral: a wild animal that is descended from tame or domesticated species

fishery, fisheries: any system, body of water, or portion of a body of water that supports finfish or shellfish; can also be used as an adjective describing a person or thing (for example, a fisheries biologist)

forest: a plant community in which trees grow closely enough together that their crowns interlock to form a continuous overhead canopy

fry: young fish

gene pool: the total hereditary traits available within a group; when isolated from other members of their species, individual organisms may produce healthy offspring if there is enough variety in the genes available through mating

genus: a biological ranking of species that share many specific traits, below the rank of family and above species; subgenus is a narrower classification of species within the same genus

gestation: the period of active embryonic growth inside a mammal's body between the time the embryo attaches to the uterus and the time of birth; some mammals carry dormant embryos for several weeks or months before the embryo attaches to the uterus and begins to develop actively, and this dormancy period is not part of the gestation period; gestation period is the time length of a pregnancy

granivore: any seed-feeding animal

granivorous: seed feeding

guano: manure, especially of sea birds and bats

habitat: the environment where a species is normally found; habitat degradation is the decline in quality of a species' home until it can no longer survive there

halophyte: salt lover

hemiparasitic: obtains water and nutrients from the roots of other plants

herbivore: any plant-eating animal

herbivorous: plant eating

hibernate: to spend the winter season in a dormant or inactive state; some species hibernate to save energy during months when food is scarce

hierarchy: the relationships among individuals of the same species or among species that determine in what order animals may have access to food, water, mates, nesting or denning sites, and other vital resources

home range: the area normally traveled by an individual species during its lifespan

hybrid: the offspring of two different species who mate; see interbreed

hybridization: the gradual decline of a species through continued breeding with another species; see interbreed

immature(s): a young bird that has not yet reached breeding maturity; it usually has plumage differing from an adult bird of the same species

in captivity: a species that only exists in zoos or other captive breeding programs, and is no longer found in the wild

incubation: the period when an egg is kept warm until the embryo develops and hatches

indigenous species: any species native to its habitat

inflorescence: a group of flowers that grow from one point

insecta: the Latin scientific name for insects

insular species: a species isolated on an island or islands

interbreed: when two separate species mate and produce offspring; see hybrid

invertebrate(s): any organism without a backbone (spinal column)

juvenal: a bird with an intermediate set of feathers after its young downy plumage molts and before growing hard, adult feathers

juvenile(s): a young bird or other animal not yet mature

litter: the animals born to a species that normally produces several young at birth

lore(s): the irregularly shaped facial area of a bird between the eye and the base of the beak

mammalia: the Latin scientific name for mammals

migrate, migratory: to move from one range to another, particularly with the change of seasons; many species are migratory

milt: the reproductive glands of male fishes; also, the breeding behavior of male fishes

mollusca: the Latin scientific name for mussels, clams, and snails

montane forest: a forest found in mountainous regions

natural selection: the process named by Charles Darwin (1809-1882) to describe how species evolve by such methods as adapting to their environment and evading predators

nocturnal: active at night; some animals are nocturnal, while others are active by day (see diurnal)

nomadic species: a species with no permanent range or territory; nomadic species wander for food and water

offal: waste products or leftovers; usually the internal organs of a slain animal

old growth forest: forest that has not experienced extensive deforestation

omnivore: any species that eats both plants and animal flesh

order: a biological ranking

of species sharing characteristics, below the rank of class, and above family

ornithologist(s): a scientist who studies birds

pelage: the hairy covering of a mammal

pelagic: related to the oceans or open sea; pelagic birds rarely roost on land

perennial: persisting for several years

phylum: one of several broad, biological rankings of organisms of the plant and animal kingdoms, above the rank class, and below kingdom

plumage: the feathers that cover a bird

prairie: a plant community without trees and dominated by grasses; a grassland; often incorrectly used synonymously with plain or plains, which is a landform feature and not a plant community

predation: the act of one species hunting another

predator: a species that preys upon other species

primary forest: a forest of native trees that results from natural processes, often called virgin forest

primate(s): a biological ranking of species in the same order, including gorillas, chimpanzees, monkeys, and human beings (Homo sapiens)

range: the geographic area where a species roams naturally

rare: any animal with a small worldwide population (or local population) that is at risk but not yet threatened or endangered

recovery plan(s): any document that outlines a public or private program for assisting an endangered or threatened species

relict: an isolated habitat or population that was once widespread

reptilia: the Latin scientific name for reptiles

riffle(s): a shallow rapid stretch of water caused by a rocky outcropping or obstruction in a stream

riparian: relating to plants and animals close to and influenced by rivers

roe: fish eggs

rosulate: in a rosette formation

rufous: in bird species, plumage that is orange-brown and pink

secondary forest: a forest that has grown back after cutting, forest fire, or other deforestation; secondary forests may or may not contain exotic tree species, but they almost always differ in character from primary forests

sedentary species: one that does not migrate

serpentine: mineral rock consisting of hydrous magnesium silicate. It is usually a dull green color, and looks mottled

siltation: the process of sediment clouding and obstructing a body of water

species: a distinct kind of plant or animal; the biological ranking below genus; a subspecies is an isolated population that varies from its own species

taxonomy: the science of biologically ranking plants and animals, arranging the relationships between species

terrestrial: living in or adapted for living principally on the ground; some birds are terrestrial and seldom, if ever, ascend into trees (see arboreal)

territory: the area occupied more or less exclusively by an organism or group, usually defended by aggressive displays and physical combat

threatened species: any species that is at risk of becoming endangered

tribe: a more specific classification within the biological rankings of family or subfamily

tubercles: a prominent bump on a fish's body connected to a spine

tussocks: a thick bunch of twigs and grass, often found in swamps

veldt: a grassland region with some scattered bushes and virtually no trees; other terms are *steppe*, *pampas*, and *prairie*

ventral: on or near the belly; the ventral fin is located on the underside of a fish and corresponds with the hind limbs of other vertebrates

vertebrates: any organism that has a backbone (spinal column)

water column: the zone of a pond, lake, or ocean below the surface and above the bottom that holds free-swimming or free-floating fish and other animals and plants

watershed: the area of land that contributes water to a single stream or stream system, usually including the soil and plants in the area because they can store water and affect water flow and water cycling in that landscape

weir: a dam or other obstruction of a stream that diverts water from its natural path

woodland: a plant community in which trees grow abundantly but far enough apart that their crowns do not intermingle, so no overhead canopy is formed

xerophyte: a plant adapted for life with a limited water supply

INDEX

09/26/07

09/26/07